When you look at this photo, what response(s) below best fits what comes to mind:
- How did that boy get up there?
- Is that boy allowed to jump off of there?
- That boy shouldn't jump off of there.
- That boy could slip and get hurt on that marker.
- Wow, that boy got all the way up on top of that marker!
- Look how high that boy can jump!
- Where are those boys' parents?

I have responded with all of those phrases over the course of my parenting years. My response usually revealed whether or not I had triggered the fight-or-flight stress response. In other words, my emotional state decided my reaction. And sometimes, I would overreact. This book will show you why.

My husband took that photo of our youngest son jumping off a marker at a beach on Lake Michigan, and one of his best friends, Anthony Schaub. I was there on the beach watching them.

Terms of Use

The concepts in this book, *Pressure-Free Parenting* by Elle Ingalls and Pressure-Free Living LLC are provided for guidance and information purposes only. The products and services are not substitutes for the advice and treatment of licensed health care or mental health professionals.

The user of the products and services agrees to assume all risk resulting from the application of any of the information provided by Pressure-Free Living LLC. The user agrees to indemnify and hold harmless Pressure-Free Living LLC from and against any damages, costs and expenses, including any legal fees, potentially resulting from the application of any of the information provided through the products or services.

This disclaimer applies to any damages or injury caused by any failure of performance, error, omission, interruption, deletion, defect, delay in operation or transmission, computer virus, communication line failure, theft or destruction or unauthorized access to, or use of record, whether for breach of contract, tort, negligence, or under any other cause of action.

Copyright © 2020 Pamela Elizabeth Starrett Ingalls. All rights reserved worldwide. This publication is protected under the United States of America Copyright Act of 1976 and all other applicable international, federal, state and local laws, and all rights are reserved, including re-sale rights.

Your Pressure-Free Journey

Chapter	Page
Foreword by Robert G. Allen	4
Elle Ingalls, Author	5
Introduction	
i. What Is a Pressure-Free Parent?	6
ii. Our Family's Pressure-Free Journey	13
iii. More Ways to Learn As You Read This Book	18
Part One. The Pressure-Free Method	19
1. Targets: Permission to Dream Again	34
2. Triggers: What's Driving the Drama	44
3. Tools and the Ten Second Solution	50
Part Two. Building the Foundation	65
4. Simple Fixes to Fill the Cracks	66
5. Feeling Safe Despite the Chaos: Safety Needs	78
6. Social Butterflies and Wallflowers	81
7. Strong and Stable to the Core: Esteem	86
8. When You Wish Upon a Star: Self-Actualization	92
Part Three. Tips for Age-Specific Stressors	98
9. Your Pressure-Free Pregnancy	99
10. Let's Put On Our Adventure Jackets.	104
11. Back to School: The Elementary Years	110
12. From Mayhem to Maturity.	116
13. "High School is Such a Serious Thing."	122
14. "Oh, Baby, Baby, It's a Wild World"	128
15. Creating a Family Legacy: Future Generations	136
Appendix	
i. Your Parenting Action Plan	141
ii. Acknowledgements	146
ii. Sources and Resources	148
iii. Staying Connected	151

Foreword by

Robert G. Allen
New York Times Best-Selling Author

This is powerful! Elle's going to show you a proven method to reduce stress fast that will benefit your family for generations to come.

For decades, I've been teaching millions of people around the globe shortcuts and systems to help them get more out of life. I recognize a sound system when I see one. Elle's Pressure-Free Method is going to help you and your family at a critical time.

I met Elle a decade ago, and I've not only watched her build her programs, some of my own clients have worked with her: elite business owners who have benefited from learning this method. You'll be glad you read this book, and make sure to take advantage of Elle's generous online support she offers you. I hope it sells millions, because the world needs this.

Elle Ingalls
Founder, Pressure-Free Living

Elle Ingalls is an international speaker, coach, author, and founder of Pressure-Free Living. A former member of the Forbes Coaches Council, she has created a series of online courses, and has coached thousands of people from age 10 to 80 around the globe. She holds a Bachelor of Musical Arts, a Master of Music, and a Master of Business Administration from the University of Michigan where she was the first woman admitted to the orchestral conducting program, and a member of the Women's Varsity 8 for the rowing team.

Elle is a professional violinist, conductor and served administrative roles with several symphonies. She and her husband Peter co-founded the Community Music School in Battle Creek. She has coached athletes and musicians for decades, and has taught financial management to nonprofit executives. A native of New Hampshire, she resides in Michigan and serves as advisory board chair of her sons' company Ingalls Pictures.

INTRODUCTION

i

WHAT IS A PRESSURE-FREE PARENT?

Welcome! I'm so grateful you are here. I wrote this book for you, and as you read it, I want you to feel as if we are together on this Pressure-Free Journey. Throughout this book, you will see ways that we can connect online to watch trainings and videos I've made for you. It takes commitment to change, and you have unconditional support and patience from me to help you achieve success.

Some of the problems I will help you solve are deep and may feel impossible to overcome. Some are habits of reaction that are generations old. And you may feel that your stress and anxiety, or your child's, have been made worse by current conditions. I'm here to stand next to you, bring you hope and belief, and show you step-by-step how to transform your life from pressure-filled to Pressure-Free.

When you read and act on the ideas in this book, you will step out of survival mode. You will be able to improve your mental and physical health and performance so that you feel calm, confident and capable.

These tools have come to me through my lifetime fascination with high-level performance. The Pressure-Free Method is the product of my continuous search for science-based techniques to help people perform well. I've distilled the teachings of hundreds of books and research papers, dozens of mentors, and countless of my own trials and errors into a user-friendly framework that gets results.

My clients experience transformation: from aimlessness to purpose, overwhelm to focused achievement, chronic anxiety to calm self-assurance, illness to health, exhaustion to exhilaration. Families I work with establish new norms of communication, respect, trust, and mutual support.

Are you curious about what you might glean from this book? This isn't a typical parenting book, and I am not a parenting coach, so perhaps you're wondering what *Pressure-Free Parenting* is, to see if it makes sense for you. I'd like you to fast forward in time, and imagine that you've read this book and that you've been using the Pressure-Free Method each day for several weeks to reduce stress, anxiety and burnout. You've been modeling the method for your child, and gently teaching it to them. You've also been making small adjustments to make sure you're really meeting your own needs and the needs of your child when it comes to not only the basics, but also the deeper needs we have as humans. Here are some outcomes you could expect based on the experience of my family and clients who have been using the Pressure-Free Method:

When you become a Pressure-Free Parent, you will have learned how to prevent the release of the fight-or-flight stress response, so that you no longer overreact in negative ways. Your family will be able to trust your emotional response much more in situations, even the tough ones. You will feel more calm, confident and in control both at work and at home.

You'll feel rested after you sleep, because your body will finally be able to renew, repair and refresh rather than spend the whole time trying to dissipate the stress hormones out of your cells. Your child will start imitating your new habits, plus you can actively teach them Pressure-Free tools so that the whole family can stop the stress cycle and start feeling better mentally and physically.

When you become a Pressure-Free Parent, you will be able to be really present and in-the-moment with your child. In fact, you will better serve the needs of every member of your family. By being more focused and reliable, you build long-lasting connections, and help your child build a foundation to realize their potential. You are taking preventive action for mental and physical well-being for yourself and your family members.

You'll have the willpower and brain power to do the things you want without a lot of decision fatigue and overwhelm. Your days will go more smoothly and you will have more time in your day for things that matter. You'll discover things about each other that you might never have known and you'll have more fun together than you ever thought possible. You and your child will have the tools to make great friendships and the bandwidth to include more people in your lives. You will have an on-going, life-long relationship with ways to overcome anything that might come your way.

When you become a Pressure-Free Parent, you'll model a maturity and a level of success for your child through your actions and your speech that empowers everyone in the family to feel like it's ok to grow, to make mistakes, to learn, and to fulfill a unique destiny. You will be more consistent in your approaches so that your child isn't confused. You'll notice when one of you has triggered the stress response, and be much more understanding.

You'll help each other as you grow together, and create unique ways to celebrate each family member's various achievements, whether they are academic, athletic, artistic or altruistic in nature. You will be laying the groundwork for a healthy family life for future generations.

In Part One of this book, you will learn exactly how to use the Pressure-Free Method, which is the fastest, most effective way to reduce stress, anger, and anxiety. I created this method originally to help students and professionals perform better on stage and in sports. I was helping them stay "in the zone." Soon, friends and family of my clients noticed the positive changes and wanted to know these secrets.

When you use this method all day long, you begin to attain an amazing mental and physical health and performance.

You won't feel like you have to drink alcohol, pop pills or smoke weed to calm down, or even get to sleep. Your child won't wonder which side of you they are going to see - the parent they can trust, or the one who's stressed out, drunk, or high. My clients who have mastered the method have reduced serious chronic disease, are rarely ever ill, have better relationships with family, friends, and co-workers, and perform at much higher levels. As one teenager said, "I am finally reaching my true potential."

The Pressure-Free Method
by Elle Ingalls
3 Simple Steps to break the stress cycle.

1. Targets
What are you aiming for? What do you want to change?

2. Triggers
What makes you feel angry, anxious, annoyed or ashamed?

3. Tools
What can you do in 10 seconds to prevent fight-or-flight?

- The Celebration Ferris Wheel
- Relax your abs.
- Wide posture.
- Long, slow breath
- Smile
- Slogan
- Flip the Switch
- Spirit of Contribution
- Write Your Future

In Part Two of this book, we will dive deeply into the needs your child has to grow and have a fulfilling life. You can use this chapter to make sure that you are meeting these needs. It's an opportunity for you to make sure you are meeting these needs for yourself, too. Then you will have the inner resources to better meet your child's needs and model ways for them to become self-sufficient. We will use Abraham Maslow's Hierarchy of Needs as a framework for this part of the book.

In Part Three, we'll look at age-specific stressors from pregnancy to adulthood. You'll receive specific tips to help navigate the various changes we all go through on our life's journey. You can also approach these chapters as an opportunity to help yourself heal any pain or trauma you experienced during your childhood; you can become your own best parent, while being your best for your child.

Age-Specific Stressors

Future Generations

Young Adult

High School

Middle School

Elementary School

The Toddler Years

Pregnancy

Our society seems to have lost emotional resilience and created very stressful, anxious environments both at work and at home. Our most high-achieving students with feelings of anxiety and depression are taking medications that were never meant for long-term daily use. There is a way to achieve at high levels without the stress and burnout. It's the Pressure-Free way, where, instead of running on adrenaline, you are on purpose, productive, passionate, present, and powerful. Before you begin learning the method, I'd like to introduce you to my family, and share our raw, real, Pressure-Free journey.

INTRODUCTION

ii

OUR FAMILY'S PRESSURE-FREE JOURNEY

My husband Peter and I have raised three sons. We juggled a lot, including our careers and which one of us was the primary at-home parent. The boys were each playing multiple sports, in music lessons, and were high achievers in school. Among the five of us, we had a litany of stress-generated ailments: we had eczema, stress acne, stress fat, frequent colds, bronchitis, stomach aches, anxiety, depression, and frequent urination.

One son would feel his throat close up when he was called on in class, although he never told us about this until he was in his 20's. Another son had frequent stomach pains that sent us to the hospital a few times. A third son had anger tantrums and felt that he was terrible at math because he missed one problem. And after producing two performances of the Nutcracker Ballet, at eight weeks pregnant with our middle son, I lost a twin. I thought we just had a normal amount of stress, and were doing pretty well, considering all the pressure we were under, and all that we were doing. How wrong I was to think that way. In fact, if I'm being honest with you, I was flat out in denial that stress was affecting us.

In 2010, when I created this Pressure-Free Method, everything radically improved for every one of us. Our sons could now trust our emotional reactions to situations. Our ability to reduce stress hormone release improved our productivity, our mental health, and our physical health. We help each other when we see stressors coming our way.

One of the first things we noticed was that we all rarely became ill. Since 2010, I've had 5 small colds, and three of those were in 2010 and 2011! My husband used to get bronchitis every year, and now he can't remember when he last had it. My eczema, stress acne, frequent urination and stress fat disappeared. The throat closing, stomach aches, and temper tantrums stopped. We've watched our mental and physical capabilities improve significantly. Most of all, we deeply love and respect each other, and our sons frequently thank us for raising them the way we have.

Hugh, our oldest, embraced Pressure-Free right away. He was eighteen at the time, and it helped his grades improve along with his athletic ability, especially his baseball. He took on a huge project of creating a hockey program for Aquinas College, which was realized his junior year. He finally achieved his academic goal of making the dean's list his senior year. And at age 22, he founded a video production company called Ingalls Pictures with our middle son, Edmund, whom we call Ned.

Ned was salutatorian of his private high school, an exceptional athlete and artist, and on the dean's list at Grand Valley State University. He left college after his sophomore year to start Ingalls Pictures with his brother. At first, we wondered if it was a good move to not finish a degree. We value education: I have a bachelor's and two master's and my husband has a bachelor's and master's. Ned felt he was wasting time and money and could learn more studying and creating on his own and with teams. It was a great move for him. He is a true creative genius as a film maker and composer. A college degree is not required for many professions, and Ned is a constant learner, taking interesting online courses.

Our youngest son William, who thought he was terrible at math before Pressure-Free, was one of the top students at an elite math and science center, and valedictorian of his class. He was a talented youth hockey goalie, and was the All-City cross-country champion his senior year. A National Merit Finalist, he is an Ivy League student: wait-listed at Harvard and Yale, early accepted at University of Michigan and accepted at Columbia University in New York City, where he is a part of the Honors Program, and has made the dean's list each semester with a GPA above 4.0. He is majoring in psychology, and is also a videographer with Ingalls Pictures, having written two screenplays on mental health that were produced with his brothers and their team for The Mental Health Foundation of West Michigan.

As you can see, we are always looking to achieve more, and I suspect that you are, too; or at least one person in your family is a high-achiever. Our family has watched our mental and physical health and capabilities improve significantly over the past decade, despite hardships and unexpected twists and turns. Our family gives credit to the Pressure-Free Method for helping us design the lives we want to live. In fact, our sons believe in my coaching so much, they hired me to coach their company and team members in a year-long program to earn a Pressure-Free Living Business Certification.

Parenting is filled with challenges from the moment we first discover that a new being is coming into the world. We all make many mistakes, and are doing our best. Just as our parents did the best *they* could with their particular set of stressors and situations. This book is to help guide you through what can be one of the greatest times of your life, full of opportunities for you to reduce the effects of stress, and experience growth, and deep fulfillment, especially in your role as a parent.

I am honored to share this method to help you and each member of your family grow, thrive and achieve more with less stress, anxiety, and burnout. It has brought so much joy and fulfillment to our family and to countless others around the globe. Welcome to our Pressure-Free Family.

-Elle

2020 Ingalls Pictures Team
Topher Groenink, Mishelle Quizena, Michael King, Hugh,
Danard Lenoir, Pete, Ned holding Riley (missing is William)

William and Elle

Introduction

iii

More ways to learn as you read this book:

FREE BONUS: You can access a video and audio version plus a **FREE WORKBOOK.** If you are a visual or auditory learner, this is a great way to enhance your experience. It's a free gift to you for purchasing this book: **Pressure-FreeParenting.com**

Part One

The Pressure-Free Method
Three Simple Steps to Reduce Stress

Pretty much everyone you know is locked in the stress cycle all day and all night, which is why chronic physical and mental ailments are so common. And why breaking the stress cycle is the key to unlocking your true mental and physical health and performance. The Pressure-Free Method is a simple three-step method that allows you to prevent the release of the stress response and its two floods of stress hormones. Once you trigger the stress response, it takes males up to nine hours and females up to twenty-four hours for the stress hormones to dissipate out of the cells, allowing them to get back to healthy functioning.

In step 1, you will be defining your Targets, what you are aiming for. When you have clarity about what you *really* want, that clarity will fuel your desire to make change occur. Step 2 is identifying Triggers. You will figure out what triggers your stress response. You'll start becoming more aware of what makes you feel annoyed, angry, anxious, afraid, or ashamed. Then, step 3: Tools and the Ten-Second Solution. Whenever you notice a trigger, you will use a tool to stop the stress response. With practice, you will be able to stop the stress cycle moment-by-moment, day-by-day, adding quality time to your life, and quality life to your days.

On the next page is a chart depicting the Pressure-Free Method. The Target Wheel is a Ferris wheel because one of the tools I will teach you is called the Celebration Ferris Wheel. First, you'll identify what you'd like to improve or change.

The Trigger Wheel is like the proverbial hamster wheel where you are running yourself ragged with a lot of things weighing you down. These are your triggers; the things that cause you to trigger the fight-or-flight stress response.

The big arrow represents an S (Sigmoid) curve with your Tools on it. This depicts how you begin learning. At first, you may not see much change, and then suddenly, you will start to notice various things improving, like you're complaining less, or your skin looks healthier. As you continue mastering the Pressure-Free Method, you can experience exponential change!

For a video/audio version of this book, go to:https://Pressure-FreeParenting.com

The Pressure-Free Method
by Elle Ingalls

3 Simple Steps to break the stress cycle.

1. Targets
What are you aiming for? What do you want to change?

2. Triggers
What makes you feel angry, anxious, annoyed or ashamed?

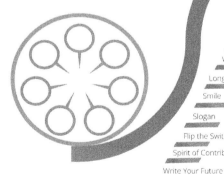

3. Tools
What can you do in 10 seconds to prevent fight-or-flight?

- The Celebration Ferris Wheel
- Relax your abs.
- Wide posture.
- Long, slow breath
- Smile
- Slogan
- Flip the Switch
- Spirit of Contribution
- Write Your Future

Before we dive into the method, let's learn some of the basics. I call this the "A,B,C's" of Pressure-Free.

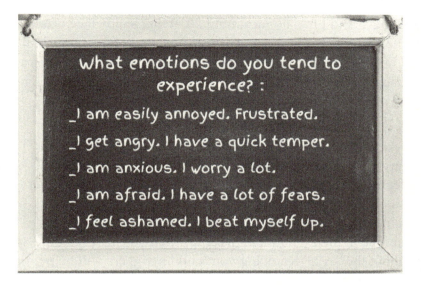

A. Annoyed, Angry, Anxious, Afraid, Ashamed

It's not just anxiety that can trigger the stress response. It's many different emotions. To keep it simple, I use words that start with the letter "A": Annoyed, Angry, Anxious, Afraid and Ashamed. These are the feelings that you will become more aware of as you start using the Pressure-Free Method. I'll show you how in step 2, when you start to identify triggers. When you look at these "A" words, is there one that jumps out at you as your main feeling that stresses you? How about each of your family members? You may have more than one. You may have ALL of them! In fact, once you start feeling one of these, it is easy for you to start experiencing more and more negative feelings. What started out as a small annoyance can turn into full-blown anger, then you feel ashamed for something you did in your angry state, and then you're anxious about what might happen next. My husband calls that, "Piling On."

My big "A" is annoyed. I get annoyed at all kinds of things! And I had no idea, until 2010 that annoyance was the biggest reason that I was releasing stress hormones until I became aware of my triggers. You won't hear many people talk about annoyance when it comes to stress. Anger is very well-documented as are anxiety and feeling afraid.

Trauma and shame are also well-documented as causing repeated releases of stress hormones. Feeling ashamed of anything can prime us for stress hormone release, even feeling shame about something you did many years ago, or shame about something that was done to you many years ago. You may notice that each family member is quite unique in their emotional makeup when you start talking about the "A's." Knowing your child's triggers will help you begin to stop their stress response.

A key tenet of the Pressure-Free Method, is that you notice your emotions, and allow yourself to feel them without over-reacting or stuffing them down. You notice them, and then make a decision about what is most important to you. And you notice your child's emotion, and instead of trying to control it, which usually backfires, you gently help them use the tools you will learn in this book to prevent the release of stress hormones.

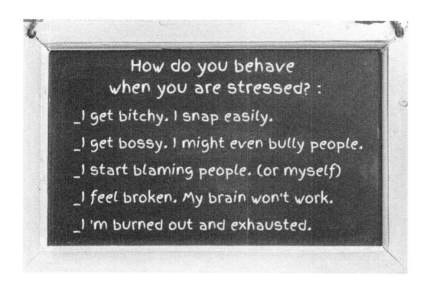

B. Bitchy, Bossy, Bullying, Blaming, Broken, Burned-Out

These are the behaviors we can exhibit when the stress hormones are released. You may get aggressive, verbally or physically. This aggressiveness may come off as being bitchy or bossy. Most bullying is the result of the stress response, and you might bully others without being aware of your tone of voice and actions.

You may try to blame someone else for the situation, or feel really ashamed, blaming yourself. Many of my clients say they feel that their brain is broken, especially those suffering from chronic anxiety or those who are self-medicating with alcohol and marijuana. Some say they are stuck, or just can't seem to function.

And many people experience burnout, which affects every aspect of their lives. If you look at this list and wish you could gain some control over yourself, wish you could not be so tired and exhausted, wish you treated your family better, then keep reading!

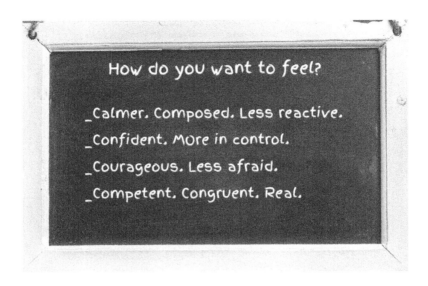

C. Calm, Confident, Courageous, Competent

These words are what my clients have told me they feel when they use the Pressure-Free Method throughout their day. How would your life change if you started feeling calm, confident, courageous and competent? When you are calmer, you'll be less reactive and will probably save a lot of time because you're not all scattered. When you feel more confident, you'll notice that you are more emotionally resilient and in control.

Remember the cowardly lion on the *Wizard of Oz*? He wanted courage. When you have more courage, what new endeavors and challenges will you take on? It takes courage to dream big, and to take action. Stress can keep us frozen. A lot of adults and children feel like they are failing at something or at life in general. When you feel more competent, you won't suffer as much from procrastination, perfectionism, "comparasitis," and the dreaded "imposter syndrome." You'll be the true you, the un-stressed you, productive, present and less triggered by comparisons and criticisms. You won't be faking it like an imposter, you'll be congruent, with your insides and outsides in alignment. You won't be afraid to say that you don't know something. You'll be authentic and real, and people will feel that, especially your child.

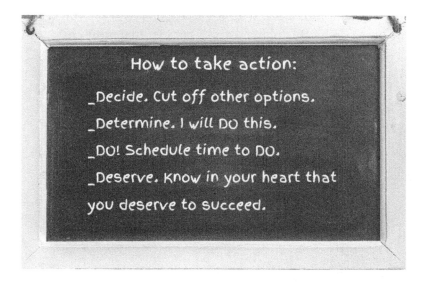

D. Decide, Determine, Do, Deserve

I want to celebrate *you* for a moment, because you made a decision to read this book. And, since you've made it to the D's already, you made a decision to keep reading it! When you make a decision, you are, in effect, selecting something, which means that you are *not* selecting a whole lot of other things. You are cutting off other options, at least temporarily. Or maybe for good. So many people don't take the first step, and even fewer people stay with anything long enough for it to make an impact. That takes a bit of determination. I want to step right along beside you to support your determination and your follow-through to learn the simple tools in this book. Then, you start doing; you take action. You can even add things to your calendar to make sure you take action. The last "D" word here is deserving. I want you to feel, at your deepest core, that you truly deserve to have a fulfilling life. I believe that you deserve to live your full potential, so that at the end of your life, you can look back with joy that you did what you were meant to do on this planet. And I believe that your child deserves to have a deep, fulfilling life as well.

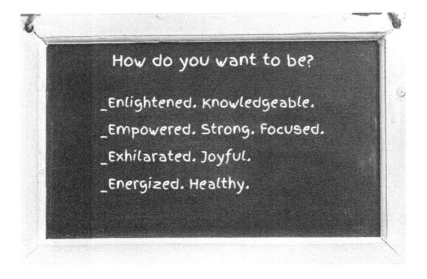

E. Enlightened, Empowered, Energized, Exhilarated

These are some more words my clients use to describe what mastering the Pressure-Free Method does for them. They feel enlightened about how their bodies and brains function, and how other people function as well. They feel empowered that they finally have the tools to help them get out of their mess of stress, to improve every aspect of their lives that they desire. By finally getting a real night's sleep, they wake up energized, and as my son Hugh said to me at age 18 after about a month of Pressure-Free training, "I feel exhilarated and calm at the same time." That's a real in-the-zone style of living.

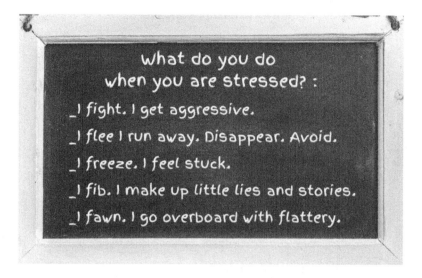

F. Fight, Flight, Freeze, Fib, Fawn (Over-Flatter)

The Stress Response. When you are stressed, do you want to fight? Flee? Do you freeze? Or maybe you make up little lies to try to protect yourself? Perhaps you fawn over people, over-flattering for attention. The Pressure-Free Method is going to help you gain control over this fight-or-flight stress response. The only reason we need to trigger it is if we are really under physical attack. But in the 21st century, most of us have habits of reacting to situations, other people, and daily tasks that cause us to trigger the stress response. We've been imitating other people's habits of reactions since before we were born, so in some cases, your habit may be centuries old, passed down from generation to generation. Or you had something happen to you that has caused a habit of reaction. What are your typical responses when you feel annoyed, angry, anxious, afraid, or ashamed?

- I fight. I get aggressive. I may be mean to others.
- I flee. I run away. Disappear. Avoid.
- I freeze. I feel stuck. I can't make decisions.
- I fib. I make up little lies and stories to save face.
- I fawn. I go overboard with flattery. I'm desperate to be liked.

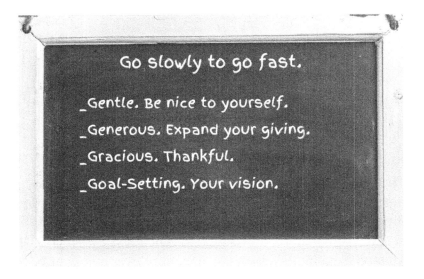

G. Gentle, Generous, Gracious, Goal-Setting

Change can be hard. Process is frustrating for some people, especially in a time when we can push a button and have access to so much in an instant. A few years ago, I was with my colleague Lila Veronica coaching at her retreat at the Sun Mountain Retreat Center in Manitou Springs,

Colorado. The farmer on the property gave us a tour of the garden and his composting process. He said, "You need to go slow to go fast." When you take your time to really digest, to really dig in, it pays off when you go to harvest. With that in mind, I encourage you to be gentle with yourself, and with your family as you learn this method together.

Extend the same generosity to yourself that you would a stranger you were trying to help. And be patient, gentle and generous with your child. Each time you notice a trigger, you will start acting slightly differently, so share with each other. You might even expand your giving capacity during this time. You can look for small ways to be gracious and thankful. See if you can open yourself up to some new ways of goal-setting that are not competitive in nature, but fuel you to be more of a contributor to yourself, your family, your co-workers, your community, and the world.

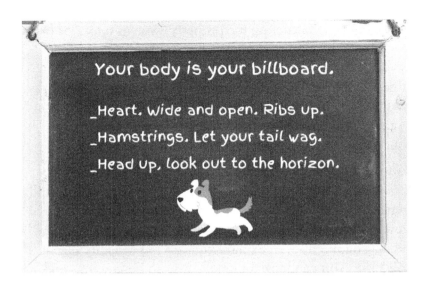

H. Heart and Hips, Hamstrings, Head

Your body is your billboard. It's your billboard for your work, and your home life. When you see someone who has a hard time with their posture, is slumped, or has a tight expression on their face, you most likely have some thoughts about them that are not particularly positive. Many of my clients who are very accomplished wish they could lose weight or take more time to take care of their bodies. A quick way to begin caring more about yourself is to build daily habits of posture.

How you sit, walk and stand affects how you are viewed by others, and also how your own brain views you: whether you are vulnerable to stress or strong and capable. I struggled with poor posture for over forty years, until I found the coach Lila Veronica. With a few simple adjustments similar to the ones she's shown me, I'm going to show you how to quickly improve that billboard of yours. If you have a dog or cat, watch them when they are happy. Their chests are full and open and they breathe easily, their bellies relaxed, their tails are wagging and their heads are alert and up.

How do people know that you are happy? These four H's:

Heart and Hips. Heart stands for your chest area. See if you can expand that area wide, as if you are giving your heart plenty of room inside you. By going wide, you open your heart area physically and energetically. People are going to feel that you are more open and connecting. You will find that you are able to connect and communicate better with others. Now lift your heart up away from your hips and relax your abdominal muscles, so that your belly is open, relaxed and long. You've probably gained an inch or two of height!

Hamstrings. When you sit, are you sitting on your butt? Most people sit on their butts. A healthier way to sit is to sit on your hamstring muscles - on your leg bones, your femurs, with your gluteus muscles (your butt) rising up in back to support your lower back. A simple test is to imagine that you have a tail. Are you sitting on it, or can it wag behind you? When a dog is scared, it tucks its tail and tightens its belly. Are you scared and tucking your tail or are you happy, tall, wide, and wagging your tail?

Head. To help correct all the times you are looking down at your phone, computer, sink, workbench, etc., and take time to look out at the horizon. Look out into the distance. It's not only good for your eyes, but is also great for the curve in your neck. Plus, when you take time to look up and out, you start to gain perspective and widen your vision, which changes your mindset as I will explain in chapter 3. Now that you've got some basics, let's go deep on the Pressure-Free Method.

Chapter 1

Targets: Permission to Dream Again

Why did you choose to read this book? Answering that initial question will help you begin to list out your targets, which is step 1 of the Pressure-Free Method. Targets are goals, dreams, visions, expectations, and desires. They include anything that you wish to change, switch up, or fix in your life. The reason the first step of this method is to figure out what you want, is because your targets serve as your fuel to use this method every moment of the day.

When you and every member of your family gain clarity about what they really want, it can be amazing how quickly the Pressure-Free Method will start creating the transformation you need to make the progress you desire.

You have permission to dream big as you brainstorm all of the things you really want in your life and for your family.

For many of my private clients, figuring out their targets is hard. Even some of the dreams they had for their children are crumbling before their eyes. And, honestly, with the pressures of work and parenting, there hasn't been any time to think that far ahead. One of my clients, a mother of four, was struggling with what she really wanted. She was drawing a blank until I asked her how she wanted to feel. And then the words came tumbling out. "I want to be happy when I'm home. I want to stop losing control of my emotions. I want to stop feeling so tired and exhausted." She got really honest with what she wanted, and we shared a "high-five" through the computer screen together!

Write down as many targets as you can think of, and then at the end of this chapter, you can pick out the most important ones to list on your Target Chart.

Targets tend to fall into two categories:

What you want. "I want…" And don't want.

- I want to feel happier with my family.
- I want to be more financially secure.
- I want to earn a promotion at work.
- I want to lose twenty pounds.
- I want to learn how to kite surf.
- I want to help my child get into the college of their choice.
- I want to feel more competent as a parent.
- I want to feel more loved.
- I want to be more loving.

- I don't want my child to be so anxious all the time.
- I don't want to get so angry at my spouse.
- I don't want to come home so exhausted from work.
- I don't want to be all bitchy and bossy.
- I don't want to have a heart attack.
- I don't want to have diabetes like my Dad.
- I don't want all this drama in our house.
- I don't want to get cancer like my Mom.

For every one of your "I don't want" statements, see if you can turn it around to an "I want" statement. For example, "I don't want all this drama in our house." becomes, "I want a home where everyone solves problems calmly, respectfully and openly."

Three Categories of Targets. Your targets will tend to fall into categories: health targets, relationship targets, and performance targets.

Health Targets.

Health Targets can be divided into Physical Health Targets and Mental Health Targets. Check out the chart on page 37 for a partial list of effects of the stress response.

Your physical health targets could include any chronic disease or nagging condition that you have. All chronic disease and ailments are caused or made worse by the stress hormones; things like heart disease, ulcers, IBS, cancer, eczema, and stress acne. If you are not the weight you would like to be, that can be a target. If you have trouble with your digestive system, trouble conceiving a baby, headaches, or habits that erode your physical health, these can all be targets. You can get really specific: "boost my body's ability to heal if I get injured," "reduce my allergies."

Your mental health targets can include any feelings, anxieties, or worries. Consider things like test anxiety, social anxiety, forgetting someone's name when you are introduced to them, or getting angry about certain things. You can list anything that you feel is holding you back from your true potential, and anything that you hear yourself say that you or your child are bad at. For example, "They're so bad at math," "I have no patience," or "I don't listen very well." Turn these into positive targets: "I want my child to be more competent at math," "I want to be more patient," or "I'd like to improve my ability to listen."

You may have Targets specific to your child like, "I want to help my daughter to stop smoking weed every night." What do you really want for you child? Do you want them to get into a certain college? Do you want them to be ok if they don't get into that college? Do you want them to hang out with a different crowd? Do you want them to stop having anxiety attacks?

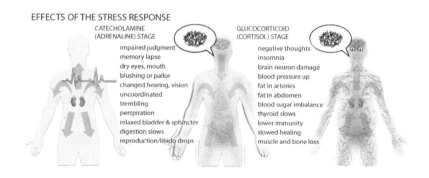

Feel free to DREAM BIG with these targets. Even if life is a hot mess of stress with no relief in sight, this is your moment to write down how you *really* wish your life could be, and how you wish your child's life could be. My client's mom was amazed when working with me not only helped reduce anxiety, but it also cleared up his skin.

Relationship Targets.

Relationship targets are improvements you'd like to see in your relationships with anyone in your life. Choose a few relationships that you would like to improve. See if you can create a vision of how you really want that relationship to be. It can help to add what you'd like to do with the person and how you'd like to feel while you are doing it. Here are some examples for you:

- I want a deeper relationship with my son.
- Instead of worrying about my daughter's future and the direction she's headed, I want to be confident that she has the tools to start figuring her life out.
- Instead of snapping at my son for all the things he's not doing well, I want to find a way to recognize what is working for him.
- Instead of verbally beating up my daughter all the time, I want to be encouraging and helpful.

Your relationship targets could include things like being more patient, listening better, showing more love, getting along better with someone, clarifying your needs, and meeting others' needs.

Performance Targets.

Performance targets are anything that you do that you'd like to do better, more consistently, with less effort, or without complaining. They can be about work, hobbies, athletics, performing arts, school, or tests. You may have some tasks you'd like to do without feeling anxious, like drive in heavy traffic, cook a meal for a party, or host a party.

Perhaps you'd like to be stronger and more fit, make better food choices, stop drinking or stop smoking. Maybe you want to grow your net worth, make more money, save more money, or donate more money.

What performance targets does your child have? Do they want to be state champions, a great chess player, a musician, a dancer, go to an elite school, own their own business? All of these are performance targets. Keep asking yourself and your child what you really want to be able to do, and some ideas will start coming.

Health, relationships, and performance all intertwine, as does work, school, and home. If you are stressed in one area of your life it usually impacts the others. The number one reason you have not attained your targets yet is the fight-or-flight stress response. Triggering the fight-or-flight stress response is the biggest obstacle to all of your targets. When you understand the role of this stress response in your life, you can build great targets.

All illness and disease are either directly caused by the release of stress hormones, or exacerbated by them. Imagine if your symptoms can start to diminish! I remember a ten-year-old client of mine who suffered from terrible allergies. At the end of our coaching program, he forgot that he even had them!

The diagram on page 37 is just a partial list of the effects of these stress hormones. Take a look at the list, and if you or your child are experiencing any of these symptoms, see if you can write down the opposite. For example, if you have to pee a lot, you could write down: *Sleep the whole night without having to get up and pee!* If you are worried about your thyroid, then write: *I have a beautiful, healthy thyroid gland.*

Notice how some of these effects impact your daily performance. If you are embarrassed because your face turns red when you speak in public, then you are not performing to your ability or being recognized for your true potential. If your child has test anxiety, that anxiety is causing a release of stress hormones that make it difficult for them to hear, see, think, remember, or make decisions. This is why the grade often does not reflect their true knowledge.

Now let's get you dreaming. What would be possible for you if you slept well every night? What if you stopped building fat in your torso and in your arteries? What if you were naturally nicer to your family and coworkers? What dreams will be possible for your child?

Once you have listed out as many targets as you can think of, circle the most important or most pressing ones, and write them on your target chart at the end of this chapter. I've shown you a sample of my target chart to give you some ideas. If you're not sure, just write a few down, knowing that you can always change them up. With all of the exercises in this book, I want you to feel free to do it your way, open and relaxed.

There are no right or wrong targets. This is your ideal life. In fact, the more you use the Pressure-Free Method, the more likely it is that you will be achieving some of your targets faster than you even thought possible, giving you the chance to create new ones. With some powerful targets defined, you are ready to start identifying your triggers in the next chapter.

For a video/audio version, go to:

https://Pressure-FreeParenting.com

Step 1. Targets Chart for _____

What are you aiming for? What do you want to change?

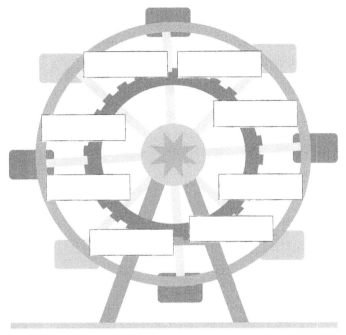

What else are you aiming for? What else do you want to change?

Elie Ingalls.com Copyright (c) 2020 Elie Ingalls

Target Chart for __Elle__

What are you aiming for? What do you want to change?

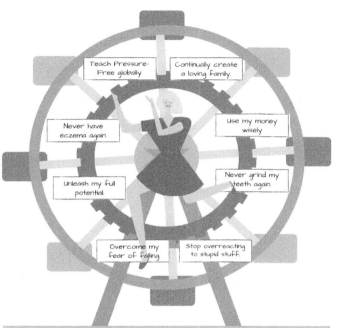

- Teach Pressure-Free globally.
- Continually create a loving family.
- Never have eczema again.
- Use my money wisely.
- Unleash my full potential.
- Never grind my teeth again.
- Overcome my fear of falling.
- Stop overreacting to stupid stuff.

What else are you aiming for? What else do you want to change?

Keep reducing stress fat, and keep from ever building.
Never have stress acne again!
Continue to improve my patience.
Be free to travel anywhere anytime.
Protect myself from cancer, heart disease and diabetes.
Hold retreats around the world, especially on Lake Michigan.

CHAPTER
2

TRIGGERS: WHAT'S DRIVING THE DRAMA

Step 2 of the Pressure-Free Method is to identify the things that cause you to trigger the fight-or-flight stress response. The easiest way to do this is to ask yourself what makes you feel annoyed, angry, anxious, afraid, or ashamed. Any of these emotions can prime you to release stress hormones. By noticing what makes you feel these emotions, you can start to interrupt the stress response and prevent the release of the hormones that cause most of your problems and those of your family.

It can be a little daunting when you start to realize all of the things that cause you to release these hormones. I was pretty shocked to notice that I would trigger the stress response at least 20 times each morning just trying to get the whole family ready for the day. Mostly because I get easily annoyed at all sorts of things. And when I trigger the stress response, I get very bitchy and uncoordinated, so I would bump into things, be frantically searching for things, and be ordering my kids to hurry up so we wouldn't be late. Can you relate? That's why the "G" words I gave you at the beginning of Part 1, gentle and generous, are so important.

If you are reading this, you most likely have a perfectionist streak, and when you become aware of all the ways you've compromised your health, relationships, and performance, it can be easy to feel badly about it. I sure did when I first became aware of all the ways I allowed stress to rule me.

I'm here to support you, and let you know that awareness and acknowledgement can set you free. You can't go back in time, but you can, starting this very moment, begin to protect yourself from releasing these hormones, which will impact you and your family significantly.

Here are some examples of signs that help you become more aware of triggers:

- Tension in your shoulders, face, or other body part.
- Sinking feeling in your stomach.
- Twitching.
- A surge in your heartbeat.
- Change in your tone of voice, posture, or facial expression.
- Biting your nails or cuticles.
- Biting pens or pencils.

- Jiggling your leg.
- Tapping a writing utensil or clicking a pen often.
- Furrowing your brow.
- Negative thoughts.

Here are some situations that could be potential triggers for you:

- Arriving late or missing a deadline.
- Too much to do, too little time.
- Feeling unprepared.
- Anticipating pain.
- A shocking surprise.
- Worry about job, health, relationships, money.
- Performing or speaking for an audience.
- Worry about things we have no control over.
- The media: social media, the news.
- Gossiping or backstabbing.
- Guilt, envy, jealousy.
- Resentment or rage.
- Being annoyed by someone or something.
- Someone you are with triggers stress, and you go down with them.
- Fatigue or hunger.
- Disappointment.
- Embarrassment.
- A bad dream or memory.

- Self-sabotage.
- Seeing your own weaknesses in someone else.

Your family probably knows what your stress triggers are better than you do. You can ask others to get involved and help you identify the things that cause you to feel stressed. The more playful you can make it, the better. Laughing and smiling when you notice a trigger will help you succeed with this method much faster than beating yourself up over it.

As you list out your triggers, circle the most important ones, and add them to your Triggers Chart. This chart shows your triggers pointing in at you, pressing in on you. Once you've identified them, we can start using tools and the 10-second solution!

Step 2. Triggers Chart for _____

What makes you feel angry, anxious, annoyed or ashamed?

More Triggers:

Trigger Chart for ___Elle___

What makes you feel angry, anxious, annoyed or ashamed?

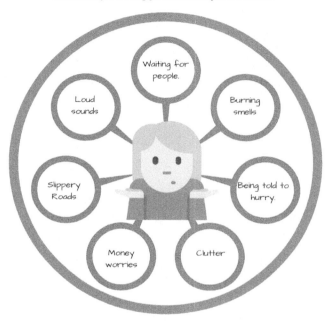

- Waiting for people.
- Loud sounds
- Burning smells
- Slippery Roads
- Being told to hurry.
- Money worries
- Clutter

More Triggers:
Technology issues when I'm trying to get something done.
People not respecting the need for quiet.
Too much traffic.
Dinner getting cold.
Any sort of sexist, racist, ageist treatment or speech.

CHAPTER
3
TOOLS AND THE TEN-SECOND SOLUTION

Once you have identified your targets and triggers, you are ready to stop the stress cycle with the tools and the ten-second solution of step 3. You are ready to solve the problems that stress causes. You probably already know a lot of tips and tricks that are supposed to reduce stress. But most of these are missing a key ingredient, and lack a step-by-step method. The Pressure-Free Method has that secret ingredient: timing, and this simple 3-step method to make it easy for you.

When you first notice yourself feeling annoyed, angry, anxious, afraid, or ashamed, you have about ten seconds before the stress response releases the first flood of hormones into your blood stream. You have ten seconds before you are "under the influence" of the stress hormone cocktail that will most likely cause you to over-react in the situation, and affect you for hours. What can you do in that ten-second interval to prevent the release of the hormones? Just asking yourself that question will help you come up with some great answers.

In this chapter, you will learn several key tools that you and your family can use in 10-seconds at any time to stop the stress cycle. The tools you like might not be the ones that someone else in your family likes, so I encourage you to play around with them and share all of them.

Certain situations may require more than one tool. I've used as many as five at once! You can use these tools on their own, or string a few together to create a system. This gives you plenty of options with which to experiment. Consider it a game, and play around with these tools.

Stress is a real downer, and humor helps. I've had to laugh about a lot of my triggers so that I didn't cry about them. So many of them seemed so trivial when I considered how much I had suffered and caused others to suffer. Imagine strapping on a construction worker's tool belt to start constructing a Pressure-Free life for yourself. Load up your belt with the tools on the next pages so that you are ready to stop the stress cycle at any time.

Pressure-Free Tools to use in the ten-second window come in three types: Body Tools, Brain Tools, and Big-Picture Tools. When I coach privately and in my online courses, I share over forty tools. In this book, you will learn fourteen tools: the basics from each type to get you started.

1. Body Tools

How can you use your body to interrupt the stress response?

Notice what you do with your body when you are stressed. Do you feel tight? Are your facial features tight? Do you have worry lines in your forehead? Maybe you feel a little frenzied and uncoordinated. Or paralyzed with fear. Some people bite their lips, or fingernails, or cuticles, or they chew on things like pens or material. Some people jiggle their leg, or click pens.

Whatever nervous habit you or your child do when you feel a stressor, you can consider it a cue to use a Pressure-Free tool. And if you can use that tool before the stress hormones release, you will successfully stay Pressure-Free! Here are some body tools you can use and you can teach to your child:

Relax Your Abs. Place your hands on your belly and relax all of your abdominal muscles. Don't worry about how "fat" it feels, just "let it all hang out." Relaxing your abs signals to your brain that whatever it is that you are experiencing, it does not warrant a release of stress hormones. That's because we will tighten our abs to protect ourselves when we are under attack. This simple action of relaxing your belly is a profound neuroscience tool that is easy to use and can be done anywhere, anytime.

Soothe Yourself. Place your hands on your upper thighs and stroke downward toward your knees, then pick up your hands and repeat. Avoid rubbing up your legs. Your connective tissue has a directionality - it swirls downward on the tops of your thighs and your shins, and then moves up the back of them. Think of a dog's fur. A dog bristles when you rub the fur in the wrong direction. It is soothed when you rub with the direction of the fur. This self-soothing motion down the upper thighs is great to use if you bite or chew things, or if you stress eat. This is a great tool to teach your child if they have a nervous habit, or have test anxiety.

Posture: Heart, Hamstrings, Head. Back in Part 1, I shared the idea of expanding your heart, sitting on your hamstrings instead of your butt, and lifting your head up to look out at the horizon. When you move into an elevated posture by lifting your ribs away from your hips, you send a signal to your brain that you are confident, that you are fine, because if you weren't, you would tighten the front of your body and coil up to protect yourself.

Long, Slow Breath. Slowing your breath is the fastest way to lower your heart rate and prevent the release of stress hormones. There are many different breathing techniques that you can research to find the one that works best for you. The key is to start a slow breath in the ten-second window. That will help you prevent the release of the hormones. My body coach and colleague Lila Veronica taught me to breathe slowly enough to feel the breath going over my nose hairs! That is one of my favorites. To really get the benefit of a long slow breath, here is my three-step routine:

1. Slowly breathe out through your mouth and tighten your abs to squeeze the air out.
2. Pause your breath and relax your belly muscles.

3. Breathe in slowly through your nose as if you are filling up a gas tank with the air going deep into your belly first.

A Large Motion. Making a large motion with your arms, legs or whole body is an instant interrupter. In fact, for adults, a large motion is one of the only ways to cause the brain to access the deeper subconscious and re-train a habit. At the end of this chapter, and in other tools, I will share some specific motions with you. Stretching your arms about your head is a simple one to start with, and also may encourage you to yawn, which will slow down your breath!

2. Brain Tools.

Smile. A smile is a simple way to prevent the release of stress hormones. The key is the timing: to catch yourself feeling a certain emotion, and smile. The reason it can work so well, is that when the corners of your mouth go up, you release a little dopamine. Dopamine is one of your "feel good" chemicals in your brain, and it also is a neurotransmitter that plays a major role in the functioning of your cortex and hippocampus. It shuts off in fight-or-flight, causing you to have trouble remembering, making decisions, and having willpower. In fight-or-flight, your brain is focused on your survival. When you smile, you give yourself the opportunity to stop the stress response and choose your response to the situation or person.

There have been some articles in the media about how smiling *doesn't* work, but just makes people feel fake and even more depressed. What's missing in these articles is the timing. Once you have released stress hormones, smiling can feel very forced and fake, and since your brain is already compromised, you lack the logic and willpower to correctly assess what's happening to you. Smiling works when you use it to prevent the release of the hormones! The key is the 10-second solution; it's in the timing. As you play with these tools, you may notice that many of the things that trigger you, when we put them in perspective, are rather humorous, so you start to have a little fun with it, and your smile will feel even more natural for you and for your child, too.

Slogan. Slogans are words, phrases, affirmations, and prayers. Anything quick that you can say to yourself that reminds you to stay Pressure-Free in the moment. Some people use humorous slogans; some use spiritual ones. My go-to slogans and some that my clients have come up with are:

Slogans:
- I can get over this.
- Stay UP!
- Let it go! I have all the skills I need.
- I've got this!
- I can get over this.
- I can do this!
- That's curious...
- I have all the time in the world.
- That's interesting...
- Stay Pressure-Free All Day!

Flip the Switch. This tool is one you can use when you start talking to yourself or someone else in a negative way, or when your thoughts are not serving you. It is a little system of tools that include a motion, a smile, and a question.

Imagine you have a light switch on the side of your head. When your thoughts turn negative, the switch is starting to turn off, so take your hand and flip the switch back on. Making a motion like this is going to allow your brain to start to create a new habit of reaction.

Then smile! Smiling will keep dopamine flowing, allowing your brain to function well for you. Once you are smiling, ask yourself an empowering question. An empowering question is one that usually starts with, "How can I…" or "What can I…" You can also ask, "How can we…" or "What can we…" if you are with another person. The question can move you toward solutions. For example, if you are having difficulty getting out the door in the morning, ask, "How can we be on time in the morning?"

The trick to this tool working well for you, is to not force the answers to your questions, but let them come to you organically. You may get an answer or two right away, and then later, an amazing idea pops in your head. That's because your brain loves questions. Your child's brain loves questions, too. Here are some sample empowering questions:

- How can I learn this chapter well?
- How can I stay calm for my test?
- How can I get accepted to the college of my dreams?

- How can we have a fantastic evening?
- How can I show my child more love?
- How can we solve this?
- How can we save more money?
- How can we afford this easily?
- What can we do to make this easier?
- What can I do to earn more money?
- What can I do to have more free time?

Flip the Switch is a great tool to use if you notice yourself worrying, complaining, meddling, blaming others, shaming yourself, or struggling with something (like trying to put together a drum set at 2 am on Christmas Eve.)

Flipping the switch can help you notice when you talk negatively to others. We have habits, that in many cases we are unaware of, and those habits can erode our relationships, affect our family morale, and derail our ability to get things done. When you can start to notice your habits, and those of family members, you can begin the process of interrupting them by flipping the switch, smiling, and asking an empowering question to help them create solutions.

3. Big-Picture Tools

Big-picture tools are stress response interruptors because they can help you stay on task and on mission. They help you realize that a lot of the triggers are rather trivial when looking at the big picture of your whole life. I also refer to them as life-design or life-crafting tools.

When you are in the flow, or in the zone, super productive, and feeling good, you are much less apt to trigger the stress response. Here are some tools that help you with that:

Snap Your Rubber Band. Take a rubber band, a slogan band, a bracelet or ring and keep it on throughout your day. Whenever you see it, it serves as a reminder for you to stay Pressure-Free all day. It reminds you of your targets, your why, your big picture. Some psychologists have their patients snap the band to help them overcome a bad habit, like smoking. You can do that, too, if it is helpful for you. I have a ring that I wear to remind me to stay Pressure-Free, knowing that if I do so, I will be more likely to stay on purpose and carry out my mission.

Double-Yellow Line. What does it mean to you when you see a double-yellow line on the road? No passing. Stay in your lane. This tool is to help you stay focused on what you are doing in the moment, so that you can be productive, creative, and efficient. It helps you enjoy time and be really present with your family and friends, instead of being distracted. Take a look at all of the things you are doing in your day, and imagine a double-yellow line between them all. If you feel yourself starting to think about something in the future or the past, pause, and come back to where you are right now. Stay in your lane!

Another way to use the double-yellow line came from one of my youngest clients, a talented 10-year-old gymnast with Olympic goals. She imagined the Olympic Rings with two sets of double yellow lines leading to them. Anything outside of the lines represents things that take her away from her goal. Everything inside the lines leading to the rings represented what she needed to do to reach her dreams.

Rocking Chair Test. When you feel yourself starting to trigger the stress response, ask yourself how important this particular thing is relative to your entire life. Will you even remember this moment when you are at the end of your lifetime, sitting in a rocking chair on your porch? This tool is to encourage you to gain perspective, step back, pause, and choose to live Pressure-Free instead of overreact. See if what is happening to you passes the rocking chair test.

Spirit of Contribution. We live in a highly competitive society. It is easy to trigger the stress response when you are feeling the pressure to be the best, to never fail, to be perfect, to never make a mistake. This competitive nature can lead you or your child to comparing yourselves to others, and find yourselves not making the grade. Perfectionism and "comparasitis" (comparing ourselves to others) often lead to procrastination because we can become afraid to even get started, and experience fear of failure.

Instead of competing and trying to be *the* best, what if you started to look for ways to contribute, to make things better for yourself and others, to be *your* best, in your own unique way? An easy way to incorporate this concept of contribution into your life, is to ask yourself the empowering question, "How can I contribute" whenever you cross a threshold or doorway, like entering a building, your home, a room, or an office. If you start modeling contribution for your child, they may start looking for ways that they can contribute.

Write Your Future Every Day. Every moment is an opportunity, a choice. Using the Pressure-Free Method to prevent stress hormone release means that you can now choose, in each moment, if you want to live Pressure-Free, or if you want to trigger the stress response. That is your choice!

When you become clear about your targets, goals, dreams, visions, and purpose for your life, using this method will make even more sense to you. Your brain is going to start believing you can live with less stress. Your body is going to refresh as your cells get healthier. What future can you now dream about? What is *really* possible for you now? Here is a simple three-step goal-setting method that you can start to put into practice each day. If you miss a day, no worries, simply begin again, and again!

If you are looking to fast-track results in any area of your life, this three-step goal-setting method is a tool to help you do exactly that!

Step 1. Write your goals, dreams and visions each day. I encourage you to simply write whatever is top-of-mind in the moment. No need to self-edit. Dream as big and fantastically as you possibly can. Your list may have items that are for the next day, month, year, or twenty years from now. Your list may change daily, or you may write some of the same goals over and over. The key is to tap into a creative flow of possibility with as few limitations as possible, and get into the habit of tapping into it each day.

Step 2. Add Two Actions. Write down at least two actions that you promise to accomplish in the next twenty-four hours that move any of your goals, dreams, or visions forward. Committing to at least two, you can add as many as feasible for yourself. This step is to help you start acting rather than just dreaming. It helps you build momentum. And it helps develop the habit of honoring your word to yourself.

Step 3. Qualify Your Agenda Items. Take a look at your calendar for the next twenty-four hours, and write a word next to each of the items on your agenda that describes how you want to feel and be while you are doing it. For example, you can use words like amazing, fantastic, fabulous, focused, in-tune, happy, exquisite, connected. Write any adjective that brings a smile to your face when you see it.

This step can be life-changing. Most of us allow all of the outer stimuli to determine how we feel. By writing down how you *want* to feel, no matter what, you are taking a step to ensure that *you* decide your emotions and feelings, not other people and situations. This helps you become more and more emotionally resilient, more confident and in control.

The Celebration Ferris wheel. Your quick-start tool is the Celebration Ferris Wheel. Kids love it. The first thing to do when you notice a trigger is to Celebrate! Be happy that you notice yourself feeling annoyed, angry, anxious, afraid, or ashamed, because in that moment, you start changing your habit of reaction and prevent the release of the stress hormones.

If you feel you were a little too late, your face is turning red, your heart is pumping, and it's clear you've released the stress hormones, I *still* want you to celebrate, because you noticed the trigger. The next time that trigger comes along, you stand a better chance of stopping the release of the hormones.

Imagine yourself running inside a large hamster wheel exhausted and stressed, and then imagine stopping the wheel (10-second pause), stepping out around it, and giving it a push with your arms going all the way up in the air. The wheel spins easily and freely now that you aren't inside it. That spinning represents your energy.

Now push the wheel again, leave your arms up high, then slowly bring them down to your sides without changing the position of your ribs. Do you see that you have a slightly taller, more open posture? Also, pushing your arms up into the air isn't something you probably normally do much, so it's a bit silly. Hopefully that makes you smile.

This Celebration Ferris wheel is a combination of three tools: a large motion, posture, and the smile. Have some fun with it, and see if you start making some progress noticing your triggers. In this chapter, I shared with you just a handful of the dozens of tools that I teach my private clients. You'll come up with some tools on your own, too, that you can add to your Tools chart on the next page.

Keep in mind the importance of all three steps:

1. **Targets**. What are you aiming for?
2. **Triggers.** What makes you feel annoyed, angry, anxious, afraid or ashamed?
3. **Tools**. What can you do in 10 seconds to stop the stress response?

As you start to master preventing the release of stress hormones, you're on your way to breaking the stress cycle! Up to nine hours for males and twenty-four hours for females is way too long to compromise our mental and physical health and performance. It is truly a celebration every time you protect yourself from over-reacting and releasing these hormones. Have patience. It took you and your family members years to create the habits of reactions you have now. Allow yourself the time to practice the Pressure-Free Method and celebrate every little change. You are on your Pressure-Free journey!

For a video/audio version of this book, go to:

https://Pressure-FreeParenting.com

Step 3: Tools Chart for _____

What can you do in 10 seconds to prevent fight-or-flight?

- The Celebration Ferris Wheel
- Relax your abs.
- Soothe yourself
- Wide posture.
- Long, slow breath
- A large motion
- Smile
- Slogan
- Flip the switch
- Snap your rubber band
- Double-yellow line
- Rocking chair test
- Spirit of contribution
- Write your future every day

Elleingalls.com Copyright (c) 2020 by Elle Ingalls

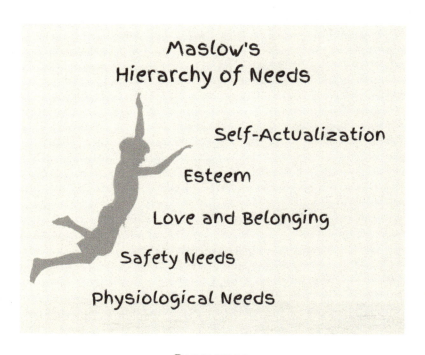

PART TWO

BUILDING THE FOUNDATION
YOUR FAMILY NEEDS

....

Have you ever heard of Abraham Maslow's Hierarchy of Needs? It's a theory of human motivation and curiosity usually depicted as a triangle. I prefer thinking of each level as layers, like building a foundation. But the layers are not necessarily created in order. In today's society, it seems as though parents need to give attention to all the layers at once. If there is a crack in any of the layers, we have dysfunction as individuals, families, communities, and in society as a whole. As you read each chapter, ask yourself what cracks you can fill.

CHAPTER

4

SIMPLE FIXES TO FILL THE CRACKS
PHYSIOLOGICAL NEEDS

Clean air to breathe, clean water to drink, nutritious food, basic shelter, sleep, clothing. These are the basics we need to survive. There is also a basic need called homeostasis which refers to the state of steady internal physical and chemical conditions in our bodies required to live. Without that one, we become ill. Here are some simple fixes to meet these needs for you and your family, and create a strong foundation for them as individuals. You're on a mission to fill the cracks; just like a cement worker with a trowel and fresh cement, you have your Pressure-Free tools and these simple fixes to create lasting strength and stability.

It's easy to take these basic needs for granted, and to think that we are meeting them, but there is evidence that we're falling through the cracks. Illness, anxiety, unhappiness, obesity, exhaustion, insomnia, eczema, allergies, asthma, chronic conditions. You can start to identify the small ways you and your family might be falling through the cracks, and just a slight change can be truly amazing.

Clean air to breathe. We take it for granted, but with allergy and asthma rates having sky-rocketed over the past couple of generations, the quality of air is truly an issue for many families. Here are some tips:

- Enjoy Fresh Air in Your House. You can open windows and doors even when it's cold or hot, to bring in some fresh air. If you live in an area where the outdoor air is polluted, air filtering can help.

- Choose Cleaners Without Bleach or Ammonia. Recent studies have proven that common household cleaners damage lungs significantly. They also cause pre-cursor cells to become fat cells. Our bodies are not designed to be around chemicals with such potency. There are great alternatives that can reduce allergies, asthma and cancer significantly.

- Enjoy parks and forests.

- Protect Your Family from Car Exhaust. This is one many of us don't think about. Today's cars don't require any warming up to function well. You can just get in and go, and warm up or cool down the interior as you go. Make sure to turn off your car engine if you are parked and waiting. The fumes from the exhaust are poisonous, and are especially dangerous to young lungs. If you do need to keep it idling, you can press the indoor air button to prevent the fumes from being sucked in through the vents, although some fumes will still enter your car. Some cities in Canada and Minnesota also made it illegal to idle near schools because they found that the air around the schools got very polluted with lines of cars and buses waiting to drop off and pick up students, and that polluted air was entering their buildings through HVAC vents. If your car is in the garage or parked next to your house, make sure exhaust isn't entering. Also, if you are entering onto a highway or going up a hill behind another car, you can press that indoor air button to keep the other car's fumes from entering your car!

My favorite button in my car is the indoor air flow button!

Clean water. Many of us take it for granted. I live in Michigan, and watching the Flint water situation happen was a real wake up call. You can put filters on faucets, and use filtered water jugs. I have a preference for glass and stainless steel. My favorite is one that purifies water at room temperature. I bought it as a holiday gift to the family, and I am thankful for it every day.

When our boys were small, if they ever started to get cranky, my husband would give them something to drink. "They just need to stay hydrated," he'd say! He was right, according to Grace Webb, Assistant Director for Clinical Nutrition at New York Hospital. "People just think that when they start to get a little weak or they have a headache, they need to eat something, but most often they need to drink."

Here is another simple fix that can boost your family's well-being. See if you can separate drinking from eating so that you don't water down your food. Just like building a campfire, you want your fuel to be free of too much moisture or it won't burn well.

Food. Have you ever noticed that even at nicer restaurants, the children's menu's choices are not particularly healthy? Sometimes, Pete and I would ask if they would fix a couple small plates of raw carrots and cucumbers, and then we'd add things from our adult plates to create a healthier meal for our kids. Believe me, we've eaten our fair share of fast food and junk over the years, but with a vegetable garden and herb garden, we show our kids what eating well looks like.

I came up with some fun ways to reduce my annoyance, and their complaining when our kids were either hungry, or said they didn't like something. Here are some tips.

- **The Handy Fruit Plate.** Have a plate of cut up fruit, grapes, etc. for hungry kids when then get home from school, or practice, or before dinner when they say they are starving and dinner isn't ready yet. I would always hope there would be some fruit left for me, but most of the time they ate everything I put on it!

- **The Big Salad Plate.** Take a large plate or platter and cut up some sort of greens like lettuce, spinach or kale, and then cut up different vegetables, and herbs in separate areas on the plate. Serve with different dressings and a pair of tongs and let everyone create their masterpiece. This can go along with anything else you are serving.

- **The Easy-Bake Meal.** I learned specific recipes from one of my clients, the nutrition coach Pamela Barton, and have then gotten creative with this particular basic idea. Preheat the oven to 375 degrees. Take a large glass or metal pan that is oven-proof, add some olive or grape seed oil, take chicken or fish and place in the oil, then turn over so that both sides are oiled. Cut up any kind of vegetables that would roast well like carrots, potatoes, sweet potatoes, broccoli, onions, grape tomatoes, cauliflower, zucchini, squash and coat them in the oil on both sides. Sprinkle with herbs, salt, pepper or whatever seasoning you like. Cook 20-25 minutes for fish, 40-45 for chicken, or until done. Leftovers are great, too.

- Children Usually Like to Make **Their Own Choices** and **They Like to Help**. The three tips above all create an opportunity for your child to choose what they want. As long as they eat something fairly nutritious, you've scored a win. You can involve them in meal prep, setting the table, and other ways that they can participate with you. If you are Pressure-Free and enjoying yourselves, it will be much more fun.

- **Traveling by Car**. Healthy snacks help. But here is an interesting simple fix. I grew up in New Hampshire, and my husband, sons and I lived in Michigan, so for many years, we made the 2,000-mile round trip every summer with kids, dogs, etc. One summer, my husband came up with a great idea. Instead of stopping at a restaurant for a meal, we stopped at a grocery store and headed over to the fruits, veggies, and deli area. Our kids had fun picking things out, and then we went to the nearest park to eat which also included fresh air, running around, tossing a ball, and exploring.

- **Restaurants**. Ask the server for what you want, and say, "You can charge me whatever you want," like my cut-up cucumbers and carrots idea. They'd usually charge me a dollar for it! Create a nice plate for your child from your own meal. The meals at restaurants are usually way too much food anyway.

- **Practice the 80/20 Rule.** Instead of stressing when you or your child don't eat so well, see if 80% of your family's food is nutritious and good for you, and then the other 20% is whatever anyone wants (within reason, of course.) I used to stress about food, and that stressing is far worse that eating the doughnut!!

Basic Shelter. In many parts of the world, we've created shelters that more than meet the basic need of protection from the elements. The one-room hut or cabin has transformed into a many-roomed apartment or house. Some people tend to worry a lot about what other people think about their living situation. They fret if someone shows up or refrain from inviting people over, if they think their house is messy. Some people spend more time taking care of their home and yard than caring for their families. They obsess over upgrading their homes and then complain that the kids are in the way when tackling big projects. One thing I've seen lately is people fussing over cleaning up before their kids have even finished the project they are working on. Whether you live in an apartment, a cabin, or a house, here are some simple fixes to enhance your family's well-being:

- Create one or two gathering places in your home. These are the ones we had:
    - The dining room table for meals and conversation.
    - The living room with rather old sofas.
    - Our "big bed" (parents' bed) where everyone would pile in for a story.

- The attic for rough-housing (also a spot of bare wood floor in the living room where lots of wrestling took place.
- The play table in the kitchen where the kids could create any sort of art or chemistry project and leave it out as long as they liked. (That table was covered in paint, glitter and glue!)
- The outdoor patio near the sandbox and swing set.
- Even a little corner on the kitchen floor can be cozied up for quiet playing so that your kids are with you while you doing something.
- A fire pit in the far back yard.
- Our huge driveway that was a part of the fenced in yard. We were the neighborhood park with basketball hoops (three heights), hockey nets, and a home-made rack for balls, bats, tennis rackets, and hockey sticks.

- What repairs are causing you stress? Leaks of any kind - roof, sink, toilet - can be really stressful and are costing you money. You can hire out the work or do it yourself. Teaching your child how to fix these things is great, too. They usually love tools. You can model resourcefulness by asking others for help, asking neighbors for suggestions of people who repair things, and YouTube videos!

- Assess your current situation and consider making a change. Is your current home stressing you out? Maybe it would be better to downsize, or upsize. Maybe you want a different living experience for your family: a smaller town, the country, a different city. We can get really locked into a situation and feel like it is impossible to change. See if you can stay Pressure-Free and neutral as you consider options and review the pros and cons.

- Get your child involved in the caring of your home to develop their sense of ownership and the need to take care of things. Be open to letting them clean and organize things their way. You can list out things to be done, and let them decide the order. Kids love to hear the word, "Let's!" "Let's make this look shiny!" "Let's do some gardening today!" "Let's make each square of this floor super clean." I have this very clear memory of my mother letting me clean the bathroom floor which had patterns of little squares. I carefully cleaned each square, staying in the lines, until the whole floor was done, and I still remember the feeling of elation and accomplishment. I have no idea how long it took me. I was around four years old. She could have cleaned it quickly, but she gave me a chance to do it my way, which was rather slow. And I've been forever grateful for that!

Sleep. Getting a good night's sleep becomes much more possible when you are living Pressure-Free and not releasing those stress hormones that can wake you up for no reason. It is difficult, if not impossible, for your brain to experience deep delta-wave sleep if you have triggered the stress response. The anxiety people are feeling today about not getting enough sleep is one of the main reasons why they can't! Here are Simple Fixes for you and your family to sleep deeply.

- Make the place where each person sleeps cozy and attractive for them.
- Pull out all of the blankets and quilts and bedding that you own, and let each person choose what they like to

create their beds their way. It could be a fun way to organize all your bedding, too.

- Use laundry detergent that is non-toxic.
- Stop using electronic screens of any kind at least an hour before bed time. You can switch to reading or storytelling.
- Remove any electronics from the bedroom except a light source, and don't charge your phones or other electronics in the bedroom. If you have Wi-Fi, you can unplug it for the night, too. Some people are very sensitive.
- From mid-afternoon on, help everyone stay Pressure-Free.
- Stop worrying about when everyone actually gets to bed, and instead, make sure that the emotional environment in the evening is calm and happy.
- Make a habit of praying or simply stating what you are grateful for right before going to sleep and share ways your kids can do this also.

Create an evening routine, and lead by example. If you are still telling your kids to brush their teeth every night, and they are school-age, see if you can stop reminding them and let them create their night-time routine. Encouraging them to be in control of their basic health, like clean teeth, clean toenails and fingernails, hair care, etc., prepares them for not only when they are grown, but for when they stay at someone else's home, or go to a camp or on vacation. You can share the cost of not taking care of things. For example, if you don't brush your teeth and get a cavity, this is what happens, this is what hurts, and this is how much it costs.

Clothing. What do you need for clothing? And how do you keep it clean? You can start with that. Sounds pretty basic, but you'd be surprised how many children arrive at school in clothes that don't fit or aren't clean. Most Americans have closets that are over-stuffed with clothing that is barely used.

We raised our sons on a shoe-string budget, so there was a lot of wearing of hand-me-downs, sewing of patches, creative ways to make shorts out of pants where the knees had holes, etc. I would box their used clothes by size in the attic, and when one of the boys wanted something new, we would go up to attic first to check out our own "store." This also fit our values of environmentalism - producing clothing takes a toll on our planet.

When I was coaching track one year, one of the runners came to practice in a pair of his father's old work boots that were even too big on him. It was incredible how fast he could run in them, without a single complaint. We shared the same size, so I cleaned up a pair of my running shoes and I very casually gave them to him to wear. He was quite the track star.

When my parents were still living, my mother would treat each of our sons to a private shopping trip and meal. They had a budget, and she would patiently take them back and forth between stores as they sought out the best way to spend that money! Once our children were earning their own money, they purchased their own clothes.

When I was young, my mother taught me to sew, and I made the majority of my clothes. I even made dresses for my mother all through high school and college. Our youngest son wanted to learn how to sew when he was ten, and he got proficient at sewing running shorts when he was in high school. He even sold a few pairs.

Cold air, unless it's below freezing, is not harmful! I see parents bundle up their kids so tightly, they are sweating. Two of our sons both had times when they wore shorts all year long in the cold Michigan winter. School was just kept too hot for them. If you live where there is a cold winter, I encourage layers, and keeping the feet, hands and head warm.

If your child has cold hands and feet, that could be a sign that they are triggering the stress response, so take some time to see if you can identify what is causing them to feel annoyed, angry, anxious, afraid, or ashamed.

Homeostasis. Homeostasis means that all of your body systems have what they need to work correctly. Your body is made up of trillions of cells that all work together. While your cells, tissues, and organs may perform very different functions, all of them have similar needs to survive. They need oxygen and nutrients, and they need to be able to remove waste. You need to breathe well, eat and digest well, and eliminate your waste well! And you need to stay Pressure-Free.

The number one way to make sure all your cells are working well is to stop releasing excess stress hormones. As you learned in Part One of this book, stress hormones mess up all of our systems and affect every cell. The only reason to release them is to protect yourself from an actual physical attack. We've created such a stressful society, that children today are triggering stress hormones non-stop (and so are you, most likely.) I know that I was! When I got really honest with myself about it, I realized that I would trigger twenty times just trying to get everyone to school and work in the morning.

The greatest gift you can give yourself and your children is to master the Pressure-Free Method. It will improve the health of every cell of your body, improve your brain function, and the function of all your body's processes. It will allow for homeostasis to happen gently and easily.

When you look at these basic needs, how you are doing right now? Are there some small steps you can take to fill in the cracks and build a stronger foundation for your family? Maybe you've been experiencing some challenges that are affecting some of these very basic needs. Make some notes on how you'd like to improve each area. Even a small improvement can make a big difference to your family's well-being.

Physiological Needs

_Clean Air to Breathe

_Clean Water

_Nutritious Food

_Basic Shelter

_Quality Sleep

_Clean, Appropriate Clothing

_Homeostasis (cellular health)

Chapter 5

Feeling Safe Despite the Chaos
Safety Needs

Feeling safe. There are so many levels to this need for us to feel safe. If you don't feel safe, it is really hard to think, to make plans, to dream, and to take action. The same is true if you are constantly afraid to try something new. That's because you've most likely triggered the stress response, so you are in the stress cycle. We all have different tolerance levels for emotional behavior. And the family culture we grew up in plays a big role. For example, you may have grown up in a family with a lot of fighting and yelling, and so you purposefully created a different culture for your own family.

Your ability to be emotionally resilient is key to your own experience of safety and security as well as your child's. Because, feeling safe is really one's individual perception of any situation. To determine what you need, you can start by asking yourself what makes you feel unsafe or insecure, and then what makes each member of your family feel unsafe or insecure. Here are some possibilities:

When someone is yelling.

When someone is angry.

When someone is arguing.

When someone is lying to you.

When you are lying.

When someone makes fun of you.

When you feel misunderstood.

When you are anxious or overwhelmed.

When you feel as though no one sees you or hears you.

When you feel like you've failed at something.

When your neighborhood has something scary happening.

If there has been a break-in to your home or your vehicle.

If there has been a big storm or tornado.

If the emergency signal in your town or phone sounds.

When there has been an accident.

If there's a bat flying around in the house!

Once you've assessed your emotions, you can create ways to minimize the likelihood of certain situations occurring, or you can use Pressure-Free tools to help you not overreact. You can also build skills in an area to be able to handle situations better. What examples here might help you?

I can realize that a person's emotions are complex and it's not about me.

I can improve my ability to communicate clearly.

I can stay relaxed when someone makes fun of me, or criticizes me.

I can approach my failure as a learning experience.

I can understand how stress makes it hard for a person to see or hear me.

I can show my child what we do when a siren goes off.

I can teach my child basic safety tips.

I can join a neighborhood council.

I can show my child what to do if there is an accident.

Safety Needs

_Safe home

_Safe school

_Boundaries

_Trustworthy adults

_Emotional safety

_Courage to explore

_Courage to jump off!

CHAPTER
6

SOCIAL BUTTERFLIES AND WALLFLOWERS
LOVE AND BELONGING

We all need love and friendship. Loneliness has become a world-wide problem for many reasons. So how can you, as a parent, experience the love and friendship you need and help your child navigate the twists and turns of their friendships? Here are some tips that you may find helpful.

Let's start with your relationship with your child. From the moment they are in your life, through birth or adoption, you are everything to them. They look to you to be fed, changed, loved, and protected. Your emotions and your ability to bond matter. If you are anxious or depressed, the consequences to your child can be lifelong. If you are finding it hard to smile, they are missing out on seeing you smile, and imitating it. This is why using the Pressure-Free Method referenced in Part One is so important. You will be much more able to connect and be present with your child, and experience deeper happiness.

No matter what the age of your child is, you can, right now, make a significant improvement in your connection by staying Pressure-Free, being emotionally resilient, and modeling that for your child. If you feel that you are in need of therapy, I encourage you to seek it out, and shop around to find the person who you feel can best help you. If you need coaching on anxiety, I am here for you.

You can significantly improve your relationship in small increments, small changes that, over time, can create some real breakthroughs. Here are some ideas for you:

How do you greet or say goodbye? The bookends of your time together at home or anywhere are a starting place. When you get home, how do you greet each other? Some families don't; they walk in the house and right on by others as if they were invisible.

You have choices. You can call out, "Hi, I'm home!" You can go to anyone in the house and say hello, give them a hug, give them a kiss, suggest doing something together, or ask if they'd like to help you with a project. You get the point. In our home, we typically greet with a call out, often a hug, and a happy greeting, unless a door is closed and it is obvious that a person needs quiet or to not be interrupted.

How do you leave each other? Some people just leave the house without saying goodbye. You can call out goodbye. You can let people know when you expect to return. You can hug, or kiss goodbye. You can wish the other a good day.

Making a few small changes in meeting and greeting can set a different tone in your home. I've seen people pick up their babies from daycare and barely look at them. And there are those very sad stories of parents, so harried to get to work, who have forgotten that their babies are in their cars. If you have a routine way of meeting and greeting, you can build some beautiful moments each and every day and provide an extra layer of safety and security.

What values matter to you? As a parent, your friendships with family and friends are important and make an impact on your child. Take a moment to write down the values and beliefs that are important to you, and ask yourself if each connection fosters those values, or undermines them. For example, if being with your child as much as possible is important and you have a friend who wants to go out frequently to bars and clubs, you may need to make some changes about how much time you spend with that friend.

Another really important choice is deciding who will babysit or care for your child when you can't. And if your child is middle school or high school age, consider what adults in their life are influencing them, like coaches, teachers, neighbors, doctors, pastors, and therapists. This doesn't mean you necessarily have to totally cut certain people out of your life, but you may choose to be selective.

I remember when our middle son was in kindergarten and had a friend from school who wanted to come and play. The parents didn't know us, and the mother called and asked to come over and meet us first before letting their son come and play. I loved it. To this day we parents have a great relationship because she had the courage to make sure we shared some values and that our home was a safe place for her son.

Watch the complaining. If you find yourself talking with friends about your spouse, partner, co-parent, or your child and complaining about them, I encourage you to pause. I have noticed that when people engage in complaining about another family member, it causes a subtle rift, most likely because the friend who is listening will reinforce your complaint. If you want healthy relationships with your friends and family, then I would think twice before complaining.

Be aware of how you are speaking about your child, especially if your child can hear you. I remember being at a sporting event, and a mother was standing with her son talking to three other mothers about how high-anxiety he is. I could see the boy's face and watched the corners of his mouth droop lower as she said this. He looked hopeless.

Everything you say in your child's presence is powerful. Because your opinion, more than anyone's, matters. The words you use matter. Notice how you introduce your child, and avoid adding phrases that might cause your child unease or embarrassment.

Develop friendships through activities. Some of your best family friendships can come from sports, music, dance, drama, horseback-riding, chess club, the neighborhood park, and all sorts of activities where your child will make friends and you can make friends with their parents. One way to model for your child how to make friends is by being the person who makes the first move in introducing yourself. If that makes you a little nervous, relax your abs and smile. You've got this!

Peer relationships are major influences. Spending time with your child develops trust and a shared value system, providing tools to help navigate the years when friendships can really go on a rollercoaster ride. Bullying, teasing, breakups, and changing of friend groups are rites of passage for most of us. Instead of meddling, provide love and guidance so that your child can grow from these experiences and overcome the sorrows attached.

Honest discussions of unhealthy friendships and boundaries help your child stay true to their values. Your reaction matters; when they share things with you, make sure that you don't overreact in shock or with laughter. If your child isn't comfortable talking with you, they may find someone else to talk with, and that person may have a different set of values than you.

Love and Belonging

- How you greet
- How you say goodbye
- Discuss values
- Reduce complaining
- Choose your words carefully
- Develop friendships

Chapter 7

Strong and Stable to the Core
Esteem Needs

Your child has a deep-seated need to feel esteem for themselves. We all need to feel a sense of dignity, achievement, mastery, and independence; to *know* ourselves. And then to also be recognized and known by others. We desire to be known, seen, heard, and respected. We conceive of the prestige and recognition we want to have from others.

From the moment we are born, the traumas, misunderstandings, failures, and other negative events can help us build a strong, stable core, or fling us into stress and turmoil. The tests can seem brutal. And yet, even our memory of them is distorted if we've triggered stress hormones. This is why many people have missing memories, or embellished memories of events.

I'll never forget when one of my young clients sent me her video testimonial. She said that I helped her discover who she really is. It is nearly impossible to discover your true self if you are locked in the stress cycle. Those hormones affect your brain and body so much, that developing a strong sense of stability and strength is simply not possible.

Once you and your child are progressing with your Pressure-Free tools, opportunities to strengthen your self-esteem, to enhance your purpose, and to feel your connection to others in a contributive rather than a competitive fashion will begin to surface.

Here are some tips to help your child (and you, too!) develop inner strength and stability:

Use the Pressure-Free Method and reduce stress hormone release. This will help reduce negative thought patterns that can sabotage your achievement. Your brain will also function much better, improving your memory, decision-making, and willpower. You'll be more productive and efficient helping you to feel more accomplished.

Become your own best friend. How do you talk to yourself? Do you seem to focus more on validating what's wrong about you, or what's right about you? Listen to what you say to yourself, and ask yourself if your best friend would talk to you like that. Criticism can be good if it helps you improve. But if it causes you to feel hurt, that you've failed, or that you'll never be good enough, it's time to flip the switch on those thoughts and ask an empowering question to help you solve the situation.

I spent three weeks analyzing the thoughts in my head several years ago, and realized that I was commanding myself a lot with phrases like, "Don't forget, you better hurry up and pick up those groceries!" When you hear yourself using "you" instead of "I," pause, smile, and change the direction of your self-talk. Gradually, with much practice, you can talk to yourself the way a best friend would. You will start to become your own best friend. You can model esteem-building talk in your home and help your child to do the same. Notice how your child talks to themselves and begin to gently move their self-talk in a more helpful direction.

Assume success instead of overly praising. Do you get nervous for your child? Get a little keyed up for the first day of school, concerts, sporting events, or tests? It's natural to do so. You want the best for your child, and how your child performs is an indicator of your parenting, so you, too, may feel judged on their performance.

If you feel nervous for your child, they feel that energy, and may react in various ways because of it. When you exude confidence and calm, your child is reassured that everything will be ok. And if you assume success for them, no matter what, with unconditional love and support, they can truly thrive.

They won't always win. There will be tough times. If you have a tendency to overly praise, or alter your voice or behavior when your child doesn't achieve what they expect, the deeper message you are giving them is that you are disappointed in their performance. Your child can usually see right through it.

If they have done poorly on a test or at a sporting event and you effusively praise them, you also begin to lose credibility with them. If they have triggered the stress response, what might be helpful is a closer physical connection rather than saying anything. A comforting hug, or just standing next to them.

As a track coach, many times I was there for a student at the end of a race, helping them stand up and walk, and I wouldn't say anything. I'd just be there for them. Once a student in a competition came over and stood near me, not saying anything. I smiled. Later, she thanked me for not saying anything. She said she just needed to feel that everything would be ok whether she won or lost.

Ask yourself, "How can I support my child in this moment?" And see what answers come up for you. It's ok to let them grieve their disappointment, and to lay the foundation for them to bounce back.

Release negative opinions. We can be highly affected by just one person's opinion of us. And one negative opinion or review can easily crowd out all the positive ones. If you or your child is struggling with someone's opinion, see if you can step back and gain perspective. What are some other people's thoughts? Is there some truth to the opinion and knowing there is some truth is what is causing such a reaction? What positive steps can you take to get unstuck?

Teachers, coaches, bosses, friends, co-workers, classmates, family members. It seems like everyone has an opinion, or we make one up in our heads! Because we are all so unique, you will come in contact with a few people that simply don't resonate very well with you. It's OK! There are billions of people on the planet to get to know.

Explore options. Your child can often feel trapped in situations that greatly affect their self-esteem: trapped in a classroom with a teacher who doesn't seem to like them, in a school that doesn't have what our child needs, in a neighborhood that doesn't feel safe, or in a circle of friends who aren't the best influences. These experiences inform what you may feel is possible, thereby limiting their options.

Ask yourself what might be possible if there were no limits. Is there a different school environment that might help your child thrive better? Can you move to a different place that better serves your needs? Are there some friends with whom you, or your child, need to spend less time? Others with whom you would benefit from spending more time?

As parents, we get this one opportunity to raise our children. When we're stressed, it is hard to plan and to envision options. You have far more options than you may think, and there are endless resources to help you figure it out. Stay open and receiving to possibilities and encourage your child to do so.

Affirmations. Surround you and your child with messages that promote your strength and stability. You can improve the positive messages you see in the day by putting sticky notes with the words you want to resonate with like gratitude, love, and confidence.

Phrases and slogans can inspire you like: *I am beautiful. I am strong. I am brilliant.* Remind yourself of your goals, dreams and visions by writing them down. Do this together with your child and say them out loud to each other. Encourage big dreams and endless possibilities!

Empowering Questions. In Chapter 3, the Flip the Switch tool has you ask an empowering question. This is a fast way for you and your child to be solution-oriented rather than reactive. When your words and thoughts start moving in a negative, unhelpful direction, you can instantly change that direction by ask questions that start with, "How can I..." or "What can I..."

CHAPTER

8

WHEN YOU WISH UPON A STAR
THE NEED TO SELF-ACTUALIZE

When you wish upon a star,
Makes no difference who you are,
Anything your heart desires,
Will come to you.

These words from the Academy Award winning song from Walt Disney's *Pinnochio* have always touched me deeply. All humans desire self-actualization: achieving one's full potential and creative endeavors. Anxiety, depression, and a feeling of failure are symptoms of an inability to experience this need. How can you create this layer of foundation for your child to experience their full potential?

I've had parents share their concerns that their child lacks motivation, and they are afraid that they've failed their child. And I've had teens share with me their fears that they can't seem to get motivated about anything and they are afraid that their parents think they are failures. That's an "f" word that comes up a lot in parenting. "I feel like a failure." "They think I'm a failure." I've failed them." And the worry seems to compound the feelings. How do you help your child develop a sense of worthiness, of deep self-esteem, of limitlessness? You've probably guessed the first step: to use the Pressure-Free Method.

The number one reason for lack of motivation, lack of willpower, and a feeling of failure is that the stress hormones are messing with your brain and your child's brain pretty much all of the time! It's a biological fact. I want you to understand that for both you and your child, if you've struggled with willpower and motivation, there is a biological reason for it! There are two places in the brain responsible for our ability to have willpower. Both of those are somewhat shut down when we release those stress hormones.

And now that you know how to prevent the release with the Pressure-Free Method, you can start to crack the code of anxiety, depression, and feelings of failure. Once you start breaking the stress cycle, you will start to feel different, because your brain will start to function in a way you have probably never experienced before. Plus, the anxiety due to the second flood of hormones won't happen. You will be using your own body to improve your mental health.

You've been triggering the stress response for years, and some of your habits of reaction are generations old as each generation imitated the last over things like a spill on the floor, being late, not having enough money, feeling hurt, or getting sick. As you use your Pressure-Free tools, you will be breaking these centuries-old habits, so be patient and gentle with yourself and all the family members doing this with you. Help each other gently when you see each other over-react.

I used to teach financial management to nonprofit executives and a big lesson from my experience was that if an organization is stressed financially or emotionally, it cannot dream or create a vision very well. Too much stress and trauma stunts growth. It's the same for you, your child and your family as a unit. But once you have just the tiniest bit of hope that something can change and that you can get unstuck, you have the ability to grow. When you start using this amazing technology that I call the Pressure-Free Method, you will be able to dream again! You will be able to begin putting down on paper what you really desire.

I have watched miraculous things happen in our family and with my clients once they have that little bit of hope that their dream can come true. When you or your child begin to feel that, I encourage you to start writing. You can use the pages at the end of this book, or a notebook, or any blank piece of paper.

Laying the groundwork for a child to attain a truly fulfilling, self-actualized life is something you can do continuously as they are growing up. It starts with being truly present with your child - NO MULTI-TASKING,2 and put the phone away. Lots of eye contact, smiles, touches, connecting, and enjoying whatever it is you are doing together will be a part of the foundation of their ability to direct themselves. Once they have your full attention, you can begin to notice what passions they have, what they love doing, or what interests them.

Butterflies. Bugs. Birds. Toads. Turtles. Trucks on the highway. Planes. Cars. Trains. Trees. Plants. Flowers. Pets. Colors. Musical instruments. Dancing. Acting. Sports. The list is endless. See if together you can go deep on any of these. For example, if it's birds, get a bird reference book or look up a bird online and learn all about it.

My husband would take our preschool-aged boys to the reference room of our public library, Willard Library in Battle Creek, Michigan, where you had to be very quiet. He would pull out books on trains and planes that were huge tomes with schematics and detailed descriptions. Our boys would sit quietly turning page after page, absorbing, totally into it.

Our youngest and I spent hours in the forest identifying turtles, birds, amphibians, and to this day, we still walk in the forest together. He also goes birding, and camping on his own and with friends.

Once you've identified passions, you'll need some more patience to do some preparation, learn with them at their pace, and put together processes to make it all a reality. Our eldest took over our entire window seat for a few years age 4-6, cutting out every picture in the sports page of newspapers and filing them by team or player. We went to the office store for his supplies, and believe me, it took a while for him to pick out just what he wanted for his very important project. He was so advanced at cutting, that his preschool teacher was incredulous at his skills!

Prayers and beliefs are also critical. Whatever your faith and spiritual beliefs are, children need a foundation of faith, values and beliefs. These may shift and change over their lifetime, but to make sense of the world, it is important to start with something that is uplifting, strong and enduring. Our family uses the phrase *full belief* when we talk about initiating a new project, or creating a new business.

To help your child self-actualize, here are some questions to ask throughout their childhood into adulthood.

- Can they do it by themselves or with me nearby?
- Can they help me do something hard?
- How can I show them that I trust them?
- How can I show them resourcefulness?
- What question do they need to ask to help their situation?
- What passions do they have?
- What dreams do they have for their future?
- How can I gently encourage their passions?
- Whom do I know that can help them learn even more?
- What needs to be in their faith foundation layer to support their future.

I was coaching an eighteen-year-old once who had just graduated high school. I asked him what his dreams for his future were. He got very quiet, and then I noticed tears coming to his eyes. He told me that no one had ever asked him that. Everyone just kept asking him how he was going to make money, but never about his dreams. Dreams and visioning are so important and critical to a fulfilling life.

The Pressure-Free Method allows you to dream. Over and over again, my clients tell me they finally feel like they are experiencing their true selves rather than their stressed selves. This is powerful. This allows your family the freedom to start to craft the life you want.

Now let's identify some of the triggers and stressors that happen during the different stages of your child's life.

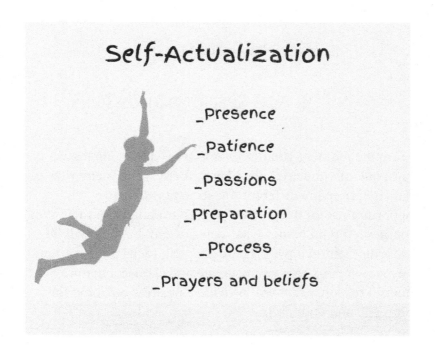

Self-Actualization

_Presence

_Patience

_Passions

_Preparation

_Process

_Prayers and beliefs

Age-Specific Stressors

Future Generations

Young Adult

High School

Middle School

Elementary School

The Toddler Years

Pregnancy

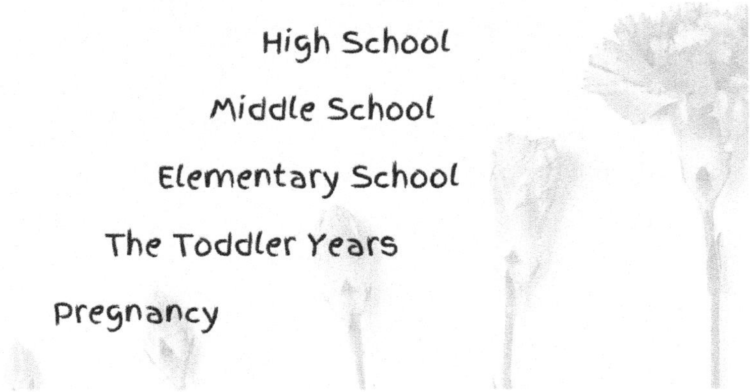

PART THREE

TIPS FOR AGE-SPECIFIC STRESSORS

From the moment you discover there is a baby on the way, until one of you leaves the planet, there are so many rites of passage, so many different life stressors, so many opportunities for the greatest joy. Your child is on their own journey. And no matter what you say and do, they will be creating their own path. These chapters focus on just a few key stressors to help you navigate and choose a mature, helpful response that will provide a positive outcome for both you and your child.

CHAPTER

9

YOUR PRESSURE-FREE PREGNANCY

....

Whether you are the parent with the baby growing inside you, or the parent supporting the process, or adoptive parents, both of you will undoubtedly have moments where you feel as though everything is out of control! Hormones, body changes, finances, emotions, and advice from others are just a few of the things you may encounter on the roller coaster ride of pregnancy.

I gave birth to three babies and each pregnancy and birth were very different. I was working full time during all three pregnancies as a symphony executive, with no maternity leave and no company-paid benefits. There are no guarantees of outcomes when it comes to giving birth. With our second child, I actually lost a twin at about eight weeks. I spent the end of December on the couch, praying that the other twin still inside me would be fine. And he was!

For many women, pregnancy is the first time that we feel really out of control of our bodies and emotions. It can be unsettling to us and to our partners. Here are some tips to help you reduce the overwhelm and feel more empowered.

Practice the Pressure-Free Method. You may notice that your priorities, goals and dreams, even some of your values, may be changing. You can do this exercise together, as partners, as a family, and for adoption as well. Give yourself the gift of a day to think deeply about what your new targets are. You are embarking on a new life chapter and your goals, dreams, and visions may be quite different.

Fill out a new Target Chart and post it to remind yourself of this new chapter you are embarking on. Next, make a new list of your triggers. List out all the things that are making you feel annoyed, angry, anxious, afraid, or ashamed. Let go of any judgement.

I remember a friend of mine, pregnant with her first, was very angry at how her body was changing. She was an athlete and putting on so much weight, plus feeling uncoordinated was very frustrating to her. With clear targets and triggers, you can use your Tool Chart to remind yourself of the beauty of the ten-second solution that will prevent the release of the stress hormones. The family can all work together to help each other for the mother and the baby to stay Pressure-Free.

Choose the advice that resonates with you. You will probably receive advice from people, and some of it may conflict. And if you are stressed, it can really feel overwhelming. When someone gives you advice, whether it resonates or not, thank the person with true gratitude. Then, later, check in with yourself and your partner. Was there any part of that advice that could be helpful? Tune in to your inner resourcefulness. Sift for the gold nugget. You can keep a journal of the gold nuggets that you feel might be helpful. Keep an open dialogue between you, and with the physician, midwife, doula, or whoever is helping you. You can ask the empowering question, "Does this serve our baby?"

Pamper yourselves! This tip is for both the pregnant person, and the partner! Take a look at your calendar, and schedule some time for yourself each week. Then make a list of all the things that give you a feeling that you live a charmed life. The little things. Like a walk in a beautiful setting. If you like things feminine: a bouquet of flowers, a plant, a pretty pillow, or a beautiful tea cup with a gentle herbal tea. If you prefer things masculine: build something, start a project, landscape, camp, play sports, hunt or fish (with a camera if you prefer.) Or, as my friend who didn't like what pregnancy was doing to her body chose to do: chop wood!

Embrace this new chapter. A baby doesn't care if you have a lot of money. A baby doesn't care if you live in a large house. A baby doesn't care if you have a prestigious career. A baby doesn't care that it has a hundred outfits to wear, or the very latest stroller.

This is a new chapter for you. And you can take a moment to deeply assess what this chapter means for your family.

Babies need you far more than they need fancy things or a new car. They need at least one parent loving them, smiling, touching, feeding, and singing. Lots of singing. Our society is seeing the results of absent parenting. You have this small window of time in the course of your whole life to be the parent of a child. When you embrace that idea, you can become creative in how you can be the parent this child needs. You may need to let go of some of your values and beliefs that served you before, and create new ones. When my husband and I married, we made a commitment that one of us would be with our future children.

When our first two were born, I had a full-time job and would walk home for lunch every day to nurse our sons. Pete was still working on his MFA in creative writing, so he was the primary stay-at-home parent for our two older sons, teaching writing at night and then eventually working with me at the symphony. When the third son came along, we switched and I became the stay-at-home parent, teaching and performing at night. Our boys have thanked us over and over for making that commitment. And yes, it was very hard to leave my executive position. But I will always be grateful that I did.

There is a small window of time that I wish I had done something differently. Honestly, it is my biggest regret. When our eldest started kindergarten, we started bringing our middle son to a daycare a couple of mornings a week when he didn't have preschool, so that my husband could have some daytime hours of work. Our son loved his Lemon Tree pre-school at the Y-Center, but he did not like daycare at all.

If I could go back in time, I would have rearranged my hours to be with him. At the time, that option felt impossible. I know now that it could have been possible if I had not been so stressed. If you feel that making some changes might be impossible, I encourage you to stay Pressure-Free and open to any possibilities. Embrace this time of parenting and love it with all your heart.

I care so deeply about you and your child having the best possible outcomes for life, no matter what. Our society has neglected the importance of children's well-being for too long, and I am in full belief that paying attention to this will cure much of the mental and physical illness people suffer from today.

Pressure-Free Pregnancy

_ Practice the Pressure-Free Method.

_ Choose advice that resonates with you.

_ Pamper yourselves.

_ Embrace this new chapter.

CHAPTER
10

LET'S PUT ON OUR ADVENTURE COATS

THE TODDLER YEARS

It was a beautiful spring day. My youngest had just turned two, and after dropping the older two boys at school, we went to the grocery store. The greeter apologized that the air conditioning unit was making it really cold in the store, and my little guy's teeth started chattering as we made our way in. So I went to the children's clothing area, and found a little sky-blue jacket that fit him, put it on him, finished the shop and bought the little coat for him. We named it his adventure coat, and I had a windbreaker that was green and blue that he named *my* adventure coat. From that point on, no matter the weather, when he went to our vestibule and pointed to the adventure coats, that meant it was time to go out to the forest. Eighteen years later, my son still wants to go for walks with me in the forest. And sometimes I still wear my adventure coat.

What seeds of connection can you plant with your toddler that will reap benefits for years to come? How can you make the simplest of tasks fun? How can you work with the energy of your toddler rather than fight against it? And, perhaps most importantly, how can you create a home environment of mutual respect where everyone feels wanted, loved, and valued? Just asking these questions will help your brain start seeking answers that will serve your family well. Here are some specific tips to make sure you never feel like you are in the "terrible twos."

The Cranky Kit. When my husband and I married, I had just finished two master's degrees in Ann Arbor, and he was about to start an MFA in Creative Writing at Western Michigan University in Kalamazoo, Michigan. We had purchased a used Chevy Malibu from his uncle, and rented a small U-Haul to make a few trips back and forth on I-94. There was construction, it was a record high, sweltering summer, and the car had no air conditioning. I was often cranky.

Truth be told, I didn't really want to be moving to Kalamazoo; I wanted a bigger city for my particular endeavors. This nagging feeling was also probably contributing to my crankiness. (Year's later, my mother -in-law shared this phrase with me: *bloom where you are planted*. Sage advice.) So, for my birthday that summer, my husband gave me a bright orange, plastic pencil box marked in black Sharpie: *The Cranky Kit*.

Inside this Cranky Kit was an assortment of things that could make me smile: two pairs of Groucho Marx glasses with the mustache and eyebrows, a fake melted ice cream bar that could be left on the car seat, two packs of Necco wafers, some fake blood, a package of itching powder (not sure what that was for, but it sure made me laugh!) and some other things that I've forgotten. The kit was to be kept in the glove compartment for use whenever one of us got cranky. It worked. Just seeing the bright orange box with my husband's crazy writing on it made me smile and appreciate him.

If your toddler starts getting cranky, chances are they need a little hydration, like I mentioned in Part 2 in the chapter on clean water. Or they need a diaper changed. Or something is irritating them, or making them feel uncomfortable. Or they are hungry. Check those things first, before you start imitating their crankiness! Wait! They *could* be imitating *your* crankiness! Take a moment and ask yourself if your behavior is impacting your child. Or someone else is impacting them. And have fun designing a cranky kit for your family!

Play together, stay together. My husband used to put two chairs up to the kitchen sink and put raincoats on our boys as they did the dishes together. Yes, a lot of water got on the floor. Yes, we sometimes had to double rinse the dishes. And yes, it was loads of fun. The boys learned how to do a task that, later, if we asked them to wash the dishes, had positive memories attached.

Toddlers long for you to actively play with them. Even if we aren't very good at their activity. I would play hockey with my boys, and clearly remember when our youngest was just two years old and said, "Mommy, you don't have any goalie moves," as I attempted to keep net. That's right. I'm a born forward.

And then there was the time our middle son was four, and I pitched a whiffle ball to him. He hit it so hard that it hit my temple and knocked me out, bouncing off my head and over the fence for a home run! The little boys were jumping up and down in celebration as I lay unconscious for a few moments on the lawn. I played outfield after that! Our grown sons have a company and take breaks to throw a football, and play ping pong, with my husband in the lead! (As I write this, we all have just finished a three-hour stretch of work, and we are going outside to throw the football.)

We also had a big play table in the kitchen for indoor fun. We never cared how messy that corner of the house got. Big projects take time, like the time our middle son created a roller coaster out of popsicle sticks. It was too big for the table, so he had to take up floor space. Quite a bit of floor space. For weeks! And I had to relax about the smell of the hot glue gun. (If you saw my personal trigger chart, burning smells are a big trigger for me!)

All the time in the world. At any given moment, you have all the time in the world. Stress hormones will tell you otherwise; they make you frantic and frazzled. Seeing their parent out of control is scary to a child. When my husband and I changed up our roles, Pete shared with me the importance of embracing "child time." We've become a harried society, always in a hurry. Things will go much smoother if you don't get all upset about time, but seek ways to flow with it.

You can prepare ahead so that you are on time for events without being in a rush. And let go of others' judgements, especially from those who have never had children. If you are five minutes late to something because your child had to go to the bathroom, going to the bathroom calmly is SOOO much more important. Over the years, I've worked with many clients who have digestive and elimination issues stemming from childhood stress concerning eating and bathroom experiences.

Patience with potty training. Boys and girls are different. Luckily, I learned from a friend who had attended a lecture on potty training that there is a nerve that needs to develop fully before a child can sense that they have to pee. This nerve can take much longer to finish developing in boys than girls. Months longer. I've seen parents be "proud" that their child has potty trained earlier than someone else's. And other parents can feel ashamed that their child is still struggling. All that matters is *your* child. The shame and struggle compound the problem.

Set your child up for success with this very natural process. Don't make them sit long times waiting for it to come; that one practice alone can set a child up for a lifetime of discomfort and bowel issues. Stay Pressure-Free when there is an "accident," in fact, I would avoid using that term altogether, and together with your child, just calmly clean it up.

Respect begets respect. The person most likely to teach disrespectful behavior to your child is, wait for it, you, the parent. When we trigger the stress response, our voices become tight, we say things and do things we wouldn't do if we were thinking rationally. In that state, let's face it, it's hard *not* to be disrespectful. If you are disrespectful to others, your child will pick up on that behavior and imitate it. If you are disrespectful to them, they may dish it right back to you, or want to get away from you, or seem stubborn to you, because they are freezing up. They also may lie to you for fear of getting in even more trouble. The more Pressure-Free you are, the more respectful you will be, and, over time, your child as well.

Let's Put On Our Adventure Coats: The Toddler Years

- The Cranky Kit and Water
- Play together, Stay together.
- All the time in the world.
- Patience with potty training.
- Respect begets respect.

Chapter 11

Back to School
The Elementary Years

Nobody told me I was going to need a PhD in how to send my child to school! All the forms, and all the meetings were overwhelming and time-consuming; plus, my business mind was constantly thinking of ways they could streamline. Then, every week there was the Friday folder with its endless packet of information, forms to sign, things to join. When your child starts school, you, too, go back to school. You will be faced with many choices. Which preschool? Which elementary school? Public, private, charter, homeschool, blend? Join the PTA? Volunteer? Transportation back and forth? A student recently admitted to Harvard who lives in Miami rode different buses over two hours one way to get to the high school she desired to serve her needs. And she had perfect attendance from kindergarten through high school. Where there's a will, there's a way. Staying open to new ideas and new solutions can make a huge difference in outcomes for your family.

Choose your school. When it comes to deciding where your child goes to school, or how they learn, take your time to choose the best fit. And if you have more than one child, it is ok to make different choices for each one. Just because someone else says a school is "good" doesn't mean it's the best fit for your child. Take your time to assess your options, if you have them. Visit schools. Ask to observe the classroom. The cafeteria. The halls. The playground. Just sitting in the principal's office for a half hour can be revealing.

When you ask to observe, do so with a cheerful voice, and be really respectful, and chances are you will get to see the inner workings. You can also volunteer. I volunteered with Junior Achievement to get an idea of what a particular school was like. And within ten minutes I knew it was not a challenging enough environment academically for our sons. Your child gets one chance to experience the school years. And yes, there can be challenges.

You may have some specific non-negotiables, and you can make a pros and cons list to help you figure out what is best. Two of our sons went K-12 in a small private school with one of them also at an elite math and science center, and one of our sons transferred to a public school in 8th grade where he could take far more advanced placement classes while also attending the math and science center. If you feel that you can't afford a private option and wish you could, try anyway. There may be scholarships available to you. Homeschooling is an option and there are great resources, including homeschool groups if you choose to go this route. You can also hire private tutors, or bring your child to a tutoring center.

Learning versus grading. Is your child learning? Do their grades and scores reflect what they know? Performance anxiety is the number one cause of poor grades and scores. What you expect and what your children expect of themselves also plays a role. When the expectation doesn't match the current situation, blaming and shaming is often what we turn to: *it's the teacher's fault, you're just not smart enough, I'm such a failure.* If you notice blaming and shaming in your conversations, pause and analyze what is really happening. How does your child learn? Are they visual, aural, kinesthetic? Do they gravitate toward pictures, graphs, and videos? Do they like to talk things over with you? Do they prefer to know the "how" or the "why" or the step-by-step?

There are windows of time during brain development where certain tasks and concepts are easier to learn. For example, memorization tends to be easier for younger children. So much so, that I've often thought that the periodic table would be best taught in elementary school. Students would have an easier time remembering it and you could incorporate looking at and touching several of the elements.

When I was very young, my parents figured out that I was a "why" girl. Telling me "no" was never enough. I needed to know why not. I was very curious about why things were the way they were. One of my sons, who is a videographer, composer and musician, would record himself saying things he needed to know for tests like vocabulary and definitions and then listen to his recordings.

You can model curiosity and inquisitiveness and show your child how you find answers to your questions. Your child will learn a great deal about how to learn certain content at home as well as at school. When my husband and his brother were small, my mother-in-law often answered their questions with, "Let's look it up!" And the little boys would go to the dictionary or set of encyclopedias to find the answers.

Become involved. There are many ways to be involved during the elementary years both in school and outside of school. You can help in the cafeteria, the playground. You can be a chaperone on field trips. You can coach youth sports, help out with artistic groups in the community, have play groups, and meet up with other families. I've seen many parents expect the schools to take over the parenting role. Your child will learn more from you and from what happens in your home than what happens probably anywhere else.

See if you can be involved without meddling. By meddling, I mean interfering or interjecting yourself in situations or conversations where your child needs to learn to do things on their own. This distinction can really help create a great relationship with your young student.

Include unstructured play. There are plenty of structured activities for your child to get involved with, and each child is a little different in their passions, so keep an open attitude and spirit of curiosity as you explore different options. Unstructured play is also important in a society with so much structured play. Hours at the playground. The old-fashioned sand lot games. Sledding. Skating. Swinging. Exploring.

Pay attention to times when you start to say, "It's time to go home now." Or "Well, that's enough of this." Parents often complain about their older children lacking motivation and focus. If your little one is really focused on building the best sand castle, go ahead and put off dinner for an hour. And don't finish it for them as a way to hurry things up! Let them finish their project. Encouraging staying power will be worth the time you take. You'll thank yourself years down the road when you have a child who is self-motivated, who actually finishes their work projects, who most likely even goes the extra mile!

Lots of smiling. Lots of hugging. Elementary school kids often have a time when they start pulling away from hugs. It's ok. Keep smiling. And keep yourself open and inviting. Parents sometimes feel rejected when their son or daughter doesn't want a hug or kiss goodbye. It's easy for you to tense up a little. Keep your abs relaxed, your voice inviting, and find times for little hugs and cuddling.

All humans need physical attention and loving. You are preparing them for how comfortable they will be loving their future spouses and their own children. I remember my sisters and I spending hours being close with both of our parents. Right up until their deaths. We are very close with our sons. And I remember those elementary and middle school years when, instead of a normal hug, they would turn around and back up to me for a "backwards" hug! It's all good, and physical connection matters.

Back to School
The Elementary Years

_Choose your school.

_Learning vs grading.

_Become involved.

_Include unstructured play.

_Respect begets respect.

_Lots of smiling. Lots of hugging.

CHAPTER
12

FROM MAYHEM TO MATURITY
THE MIDDLE SCHOOL YEARS

Do you remember your middle school or junior high years? For most of us, there was quite a bit of chaos and drama. These years tend to be where helicopter parenting, "tiger" parenting, and other habits of parenting get established. When our sons reached middle school, I took the approach of creating more independence for them. I did not look at their grades on the school apps, and told each boy that it was their responsibility to let me know if they needed some help or if they felt they hadn't done as well as they could on something. It was the right approach for our sons. They flourished without my interference. Things got even better in 2010 when I created the Pressure-Free Method. Our youngest had an even better middle school experience than our older two sons, since my husband and I reduced our overreacting significantly. None of them experienced the chaos that I did when I was that age, but there will always be challenges as you navigate puberty.

I'll never forget when our middle son said how lucky our youngest was to have Pressure-Free, and also, to be able to trust his parents' emotional reactions to situations and challenges. Not that we were perfect by any means, but the difference was palpable to him. That being said, you might need to load up your Pressure-Free tool belt and strap it on for these years!

Stay on the same page. Both parents need to really communicate and work to stay on the same page during this time. So does the whole family. When you and your child find ways to stay on the same page, united and connected, you can make this one of the most fun, rewarding times. Just like in the toddler years, keep finding ways to do things together.

A united, stable, nurturing, loving home life is more important than ever as your middle-schooler navigates their own body changes, bullying, emotions, friendships changing, and "mean" kids (both boys and girls). Rituals and routines that keep you talking, having fun together, and solving problems together can help you stay on the same page. Look for ways to establish them. Share some of your challenges from when you were that age. You can even share how you may have been afraid to tell your parents things. And watch out for bullying and mean behavior which is our next subject.

Overcoming bullying. I've never seen anyone not be mean at least a little bit. Especially if they've triggered the stress response. That's when bitchiness, bossiness, bullying, and blaming really start to be exhibited. If your child is afraid, they may lash out and be mean to others. Creating a safe place at home to talk about what is happening at school, in sports, or other activities is the first step to untangling what's really going on.

It's hard for any of us to own up to certain behaviors. I had some really scary things happen to me when I was young. I was so afraid of it all, that I never told anyone about it. This happens to a lot of people. You can probably assume that your child is learning to deal with something on their own which could explain their behavior if they seem stressed.

I also don't think I ever told my parents a really awful experience in junior high. I was getting changed into my cheerleader outfit in the girls' locker room, and someone made fun of my multi-colored bikini underwear (most girls had big plain, white underwear back then.) Before I had time to put my navy bloomers on over my underwear, four girls grabbed my arms and legs and pulled me out into the gym with my skirt up so that everyone in the stands could see my underwear. Horrifying and humiliating. When they dropped me on the floor of the locker room, I kept a stiff upper lip, put my bloomers on, and went out there and cheered as if nothing had happened.

I don't remember which four girls it was. I don't remember feeling like I had to retaliate. I do remember thinking that, in general, you can't really trust other people and that you have to be strong. The event definitely made me wary.

Things are going to happen to your kids. Nurture and guide. And let them know that you are on the same page and a safe haven for them.

Embrace the body changes. Whether you're ready for it or not, your child is going to go through the mayhem of puberty and become physically mature, which means capable of reproducing. Your child might bloom early, or they might be a late bloomer. Regardless of when their bodies start going through this big change, how you approach it can make a huge difference in their self-esteem, and their fear level.

Our three sons started school a year earlier than some of their classmates, so when middle school came, many of their friends were much taller than they were. Height, strength, hair, breast size, penis size, voice changes, smells, the need for a bra, the need to shave, the need for "deodorizer," as our middle son still calls it, are all open for discussion. Keep as many avenues open for these discussions as possible. What they learn on the street from their peers may be incorrect and even harmful. Your talks don't have to be heavy necessarily. You can have humorous moments, serious moments, and tender moments as you navigate this time.

Keep a Dreams List. I remember a research study back in the late 80's that had female junior high students write down all their goals and dreams for the next five years. Not one of the girls wrote that she wanted to have sex, get pregnant or do drugs. When you take time with your child and have them write out their goals and dreams, you have a starting place in case things start to go off track a little bit. (Or a lot.)

Some people find visualization a challenge, so you may want to look at magazines or photos on line for inspiration. Build a Pinterest page or a vision board that you can hang up. What kind of house do they want to live in? Where would they like to travel? What languages would they like to learn? What do they want to do well? What do they want to learn more about? What colors do they like? What fonts? Who is a hero or heroine to them? You can do this once or twice a year, or each season. I put my vision board right on my bathroom mirror to remind me every day of where I'm headed.

Be aware of potential embarrassment. Is there something that you do that embarrasses your child? Is your clothing appropriate when you attend a school function? Do you over-dress? If you are creating a good flow of communication, you can ask your child their opinion to minimize any embarrassment. Your feelings matter, too. I remember sitting with my parents for my school awards ceremony, and a dear friend asking if she could sit with us because her daughter didn't want to sit with her, but wanted to be with a group of friends.

I was so happy to have this woman sit with me that night, especially when I could see that she was a little hurt and vulnerable. It wouldn't have crossed my mind to not sit with my parents. But then I realized that some kids, for a variety of reasons, might not want to.

Enjoy your drives together. You may have to spend time driving your child around, or riding public transportation with them to events and friends' houses. You can use the drives to have great conversations, which can seem easier when you are both looking forward on the road. You can create different games to play and songs to sing while driving. And you can have work, a craft, or a book to pass the time if you foresee waiting for your child.

My mother knit a lot of sweaters and read a lot of mysteries waiting in the car for our violin and cello lessons. And in the summer, we'd stop for a little treat at a restaurant after our lessons. She made it fun. Try not to complain about having to drive your children places. Soon they will be driving themselves and you'll wish you could go back to your rides together!

From Mayhem to Maturity
The Middle School Years

_Stay on the same page.

_Overcoming bullying.

_Embrace body changes.

_Keep a Dreams List.

_Be aware of potential embarrassment

_Enjoy your drives together.

CHAPTER
13

"HIGH SCHOOL IS SUCH A SERIOUS THING.
THESE PROBLEMS MATTER."

High school is such a serious thing. These problems matter. This is a quote from an episode of *Family Guy*. A show that you, like me, may not necessarily approve of, but this episode has been watched millions of times, and kids quote it. The episode pokes fun at teenage angst, and in doing so, highlights the real things affecting teens. When people talk about their high school years, there is such a wide range of experiences, emotions, and memories. Some people loved it. Some hated it. The kind of experience you had can have an impact on what you think is possible for your child. See if you can widen your vision about what this time can be like for your child. These problems do matter. And over-reacting to them can make them worse. Staying Pressure-Free and finding solutions are critical.

Be there. A letter had come in the mail for my son from the National Merit Scholarship office. That same day, a mother of a student at Marjory Stoneham Douglas High School in Florida had received a similar letter. I couldn't wait for my son to get home from school and open that letter that told him that he wasn't just a semi-finalist, he was a finalist for the National Merit Scholarship. So was the student in Florida, but she would never open that letter. She lost her life the day before in that tragic school shooting of 2018.

Over the years, we've had lots of talks around our dining room table about mental health, violence, and how many students live on the edge. Navigating the high school years requires your presence, your love and your guidance. It's tempting for parents to add more work outside the home during these years, especially with the cost of college looming.

I encourage you, if at all possible, to create schedules that allow a parent to be home when your child is home. And to create a warm environment where your child's friends want to be. It really is important to be there. And to have plenty of flexibility with schedules to accommodate all of the extra activities your child is engaged in. Attend. Enjoy. Stay Pressure-Free as you watch them so that they can trust your energy, and your reaction to their performance.

Ask empowering questions. There is so much out of your control as a parent when your student hits high school. And so much peer influence. It is never too late to make some changes, though. Here are some empowering questions to ask:

- How can we solve this?
- What is the best course of action?
- Who can help us?
- How can I stay calm in this situation?
- What does my child need?
- What is the best environment for my child?

And stay open to lots of possibilities. Stay open to asking for help, counseling, coaching. Stay open to exploring changing schools. Let the answers to your questions come to you organically. Some things will be out of your control. Notice what you *can* control, what you *can* influence. Especially watch your reactions to situations, and make sure you use Pressure-Free tools to stay calm and composed so that you choose your response rather than overreact. Your child will trust you so much more if you provide stability for them.

Awareness of Substance Abuse. It starts with you. One of the best gifts you can give your child is to not disappear into alcohol, pills or marijuana. A drunk or stoned parent cannot properly care for a child. Your child won't be able to trust your responses if you regularly use substances that alter your behavior and emotions. If you find yourself needing to escape, to run from your problems, see if you can get the help you need for yourself and for your child's sake. Regardless of your behavior regarding substances, your child will be navigating their choices starting anywhere from elementary age to college age.

Another great gift you can give your child is to stay emotionally resilient with the Pressure-Free Method. Overreaction to situations, yelling, fighting, and violence rarely leads to solutions. Your child is much more apt to listen to you if you state clearly what you think about a situation.

You might say or hear that all kids experiment with drugs and alcohol, but that's not true. They all don't. In fact, I've met students who have never touched any substances because they don't want to be like their parents who are substance abusers. They want to break the cycle. I have never smoked anything, nor done cocaine, which was very popular during my college years. I took a few sips of alcohol in high school, and some the summer of my twenty-first birthday, but had very little alcohol at any time until age forty when I stopped nursing my last baby.

Watch out for marijuana. There are strains that are very potent. And there seems to be a subset of the population who use it and experience serious psychosis from just one experience. States that have legalized are seeing younger and younger children getting access to it to smoke and also access to edibles. Some of the psychosis leads to violence. I have had several clients in their 20's who come to me with weed issues and want to stop. Many wish they'd never even tried it.

At the first sign that your child might be regularly doing any sort of drug, seek help. Even parents trained in social work and mental health know that extra help is needed. Stay Pressure-Free, and stay open to conversations so that together you can find solutions. Force and judgement usually backfire, and can drive behavior underground.

If a child of yours is really struggling and you have other children, make sure that you actively spend time with each of them. It is easy to neglect children who seem to have it all together and are doing well. But if one of their siblings is having a rough time, they are probably feeling confused and scared about what is happening, particularly if parents are fighting over what to do. Substance abuse by anyone in the family is one of the toughest things to navigate and one of the most destructive in terms of meeting the needs of a child, including the children who are not abusing substances.

Puberty and sex. Going through puberty is such a rite of passage. If a child has at least one parent or adult whom they can talk to about all of the changes and feelings, it can be so helpful. Many kids learn from their peers and the information can be pretty sketchy. Educate yourself. There are plenty of resources to help you, especially with the high levels of serious sexually transmittable diseases today. You can make sure they feel comfortable talking with their doctor, counselor, pastor or therapist as well.

Make time for connection. Play! Let your inner kid out! Find some common activities that provide fun, adventure and a chance to experience each other's company. Each one of my sons and I had a favorite card game the two of us played. Hugh and I played double solitaire. Ned and I played cribbage. William and I played rummy.

Recently, when my husband and I moved to a new home, we started playing double solitaire every night after dinner, and whoever eats with us plays, too. We even have special cards one of our sons and his girlfriend bought at a gas station for Christmas that we save for when all six of us play solitaire. One of our sons just recently learned that you can play solitaire by yourself; he assumed it was a game for two or more players! We also keep footballs, frisbees, tennis racquets and other assorted games for use at any time. The family who plays together, stays together!

High school is such a serious thing. These problems matter.

_Be there.

_Ask empowering questions.

_Awareness of substance abuse.

_Puberty and sex.

_Make time for connection. Play!

CHAPTER

14

"Oh, Baby, Baby, It's a Wild World"

Young Adult

Technically, your child is an adult. But are they ready? The Cat Stevens song I reference in this chapter title is pretty accurate. I went out into the world thinking that people have good intentions. Some do not. I was naive, and I got hurt on a number of occasions. But the challenges made me a survivor and helped me empathize with others who have crap happen to them along the way. Three things I've always had an abundance of are discipline, drive, and focus. What skills and values does your young adult have? And how can you be there for them without meddling?

Be a Safety Net. Be a safety net, rather than a helicopter parent. What can you provide your child in terms of a safety net when they leave home, go to college, or start working full time? You can provide some emotional stability for them by being a good listener. You can let them know that if things get tough, they can come home for a visit to re-group. Be straight-up with them about money and expectations. Most of all, you can have adult conversations and treat them with the respect you would other adults.

I chose to go to college 1000 miles away from home. I had never been on a jet. I'd never been west of Vermont! My mother flew with me to Michigan and we packed up four suitcases of my belongings with a small space for her change of clothes. When we left Boston's airport and were high in the air, she turned to me and said, "Well, Pamela, you are off on your adult adventure now. You can come visit us, but you will never live with us again." There wasn't much to say back but, "OK."

My mother cut the apron strings at what was one of the most exciting and terrifying times of my life. And I'm glad she did. We visited my folks in New Hampshire. But I never did live there again. And honestly, I'm glad she was so forthright in her belief in me to make my way in the world. Yes, there were times when I was homesick, and sometimes I have a pang of heartsickness that I missed time with them. But over the years, we had fantastic times with my parents, especially when our babies came along.

You can give your child the space they need to create their family with their spouse. Many parents hover, and it can cause difficulties. Our first baby was due in March, and when the holidays came, I didn't feel comfortable traveling pregnant. I'll never forget talking to my mom about it and she said, "You're building your own family now. You don't ever need to feel pressure to be in New Hampshire for the holidays. You're now creating your own traditions." My parents gave my two sisters and me space to live our lives in far away places, and they also gave us a safety net of love, nurturing, and belief in our abilities that I still feel, even though they both passed away in 2005.

Vocations and Avocations. What is your primary work, and what are other passions that you enjoy that are side hustles or hobbies? What careers can you expose your children to? Some children seem to know from a young age what their life's calling is. Others take a while. Some people never really do find the best fit. How about you? Your work experience, paid or unpaid, and how you feel about it, will influence your child.

It may take a while after high school for them to find their life's work. I've heard parents say things like *college is a waste if the kid doesn't know what they want to do.* I disagree. Finding out what they *don't* want to do can be a valuable way to discover what they *do* want to do. And in my opinion, learning is never a waste of time or money. The accounting class they took may come in handy when they do their tax return!

When you value all work, and all studying, your child will feel supported as they explore. Find something positive in your child's exploration to encourage them to keep searching. It's not so much what we do in life, but how we do it that creates fulfillment.

Patience with the process. Sometimes it takes a while for a young person to find their vocation. If your child hasn't been exposed to many options, it may take some time and exploration for them to land. Many adults are still searching. It took my husband several years, and several schools before he completed his undergraduate degree. When I met him, he had the highest SAT score of anyone I knew and he was a junior in engineering at the University of Michigan. He had great math and science skills like his father, who was an engineer, but he was not happy in that field. He left at the end of that year, worked in a factory, went to a community college, went to France, then went to Saginaw Valley State University to study business.

At Saginaw, where he was editor of the school paper, one of his professors praised his writing, and encouraged him to go back to the University of Michigan and get a degree in English. He did, and won a Hopwood Award for a collection of poetry. He then won a scholarship to get his MFA in Creative Writing at Western Michigan University. He taught at the college level, worked in a book store, sold Cut-Co knives was a stay-at-home Dad, founded a music school with me, worked with me as a Marketing Director, worked at a hardware store, managed an ice-cream shop one summer, and now works as a Marketing Strategist with our sons' company. He is an amazingly creative person. I am sure his Magnus Opus is percolating and will one day be written.

High achievers want to do it all. With the high level of anxiety on college campuses today, there is talk of making certain graduate programs easier. I don't believe that will work. A high achieving student will add another degree or take on more part-time jobs if the work isn't challenging enough. High achievers have a wide bandwidth, with a lot of abilities that they feel compelled to use. This is why Pressure-Free is the perfect stress management program for high achievers; you can reduce stress and anxiety without slowing down or taking time off. You can do more because you aren't tired, and you can be much more productive because your brain and body are functioning at a higher level.

I understand high achievers, because I've been one my whole life. From the time I was small, if someone told me, "No," I would find a way. I would always add one more activity, one more club, one more course, one more sewing project. When someone told me to slow down, I would work even harder.

At the University of Michigan, I started out studying physical education and music education, and taking honors classes. I won a seat in the Varsity 8 for the rowing team my first year, was assistant concertmaster of the orchestra for non-music majors, and was named one of the Branstrom Prize winners for highest GPA.

After one semester, I knew I wanted to go full time into music. I also wanted to study violin with a professor who only took performance majors. When I was told by the registrar that I could not study with him, I went down the hall, knocked on his door and played for him. I'm sure my playing was far from that of his usual student, but he said he loved my chutzpah and wrote a letter that permitted me to study with him. Two years later, I was mentored by a conductor and changed my major again entering a special program where I could design my own curriculum which included violin performance, French, and graduate conducting courses.

Two years after my undergrad, after diligent studying, including a summer at the Mozarteum in Salzburg, I was accepted into both the MBA program and the Orchestral

Conducting program at the University of Michigan as the first woman. All the time I was in college, I had jobs: teaching gymnastics and track to small children, working in a deli, selling Tupperware, two library jobs, lots of professional symphony jobs, violin gigs, restaurant jobs, bank teller, orchestra manager, assistant conductor.

After college I was a waitress, a conductor of a youth orchestra, a marketing director of a symphony, an executive director of a symphony, an artist manager, co-founder of a music school, financial consultant, track coach, college professor, marketing executive for an online store, and stay-at-home mother. Now I'm chair of the advisory board of our sons' company and CEO and Founder of Pressure-Free Living. I'm an author, speaker, and high-performance coach. Every job I ever had was valuable, and taught me so much.

What's your story? What are all the jobs you've had in your life? Share your journey with your adult child. Let them know that all work has validity, including minimum wage and server jobs. Supporting oneself and one's family is laudable. Making ends meet, no matter what, *is* empowering.

Define success. How do you define success? How did your parents? How does your child? If you and your child each make a list of all the things that make up your definition of success and prioritize it, you will see where you are similar and where you are different. For example, a person who isn't interested in team sports can have a hard time understanding why playing a sport is so important.

I can still see the confused expression on my high school guidance counselor's face when he told me of how successful I will be in an engineering career, and I told him that I wanted to conduct orchestras and coach athletes. He didn't understand that at the age of 10, I decided that I would be a professional violinist, and that Archangelo Corelli and Antonio Vivaldi were my heroes! This mattered to me!

As we raised our boys, we began defining success in terms of fulfillment, encouraging our boys to explore what they were passionate about. Film-making was at the top of the list. Their Batman movie they made was a favorite we've watched many times. Lots of sports. All three boys played travel hockey, baseball, basketball, football, and ran track and cross-country. Lots of music. Ned is an accomplished guitarist, pianist and composer. Hugh joined the Battle Creek Boychoir, not necessarily because he wanted to sing, but because it was one of the most "excellent" things to do in our city, and he would get to tour other cities and countries. William had been making films since he was very young, and has a great knowledge of classical music; Sibelius' Third Symphony was his hockey pump-up song.

We taught our boys to dream, and then work to make those dreams a reality. We taught them this by modeling. When Pete and I wanted to create a music school for our city, more than one city leader told us it would never fly. The boys watched us work for over a year, winning a national grant, collaborating with city leaders who *did* believe in us, auditioning faculty, looking for facilities. We created that school, which has since served thousands of people of all ages and socio-economic backgrounds.

Hugh dreamed of playing college hockey but wanted to go to a college that didn't have a team, so for three years he worked and collaborated to build one, getting to play his junior and senior years. Ned and his friend designed and built a boat made out of duct tape. They brought it on our boat trailer to Lake Michigan and sailed it. If you google our old address: 153 Laurel Drive, Battle Creek, Michigan, you will see it sitting in the front lawn! William wanted to learn to sew at age 10, and made a maroon, crushed-velvet, silver-backed vest and black crushed-velvet knickers. He designed a dress for me that we made together and then he learned to waltz and taught me!

What dreams does your child have? Do you support them? Do you assume success for them, even when other people think they're impossible?

"Oh, baby, baby it's a wild world. Young adult.

_Be a safety net.

_Vocations and avocations.

_Patience with the process.

_High achievers want to do it all.

_Define success.

CHAPTER

15

CREATING A FAMILY LEGACY
THE FUTURE GENERATIONS

We were driving back from seeing my mother-in-law and celebrating Fathers' Day. Ned, our middle son, with his driver's permit was at the helm of the van. Our eldest, Hugh, was in the passenger seat, and my husband and I were flanking our youngest, Willam, in the back.

My husband had just brainstormed a name for this method I was creating, and we decided on a play on my initials PSI, pounds-per-square-inch. Pressure. Pressure-Free. Our eldest, 18-years-old at the time, was using the method all day, every day, and as we drove home that day, he turned around and looked at me and said, "Mother, I can't wait to be married and have a family and share the legacy of how we live now." He was comparing how we were before Pressure-Free to how we now seemed to effortlessly solve problems and communicate and interact; how fulfilling our lives are.

The legacy of how we live... I can still feel how the tears welled up in my eyes when he said that. I think that most people connect the idea of family legacy with inheritance, with money. But he was talking about *how* we live. It was one of the most inspiring moments of my life.

How *do* you want to live? How do you want your family to live? What sort of generational legacy are you leaving? A question that comes up in my mind is what stressors are in the way of creating your family legacy and how can you overcome them? That's an empowering question that can help you get started. Here are some tips to help you be forward-thinking.

Developing financial success. What does your child know about money? What have you taught them or modeled for them? Is there a lot of complaining about money? Do they over-spend? Are they in the habit of saving? A lot of families fight about money, and children grow up feeling tense about financial matters. You can make a change to talk about money calmly and model behavior that could help your child.

If you are financially successful, your child might feel that they could never attain the same success, or they may feel that you will always take care of them if they flounder.

If you are struggling financially, and you need to learn more and change some habits, consider learning together.

Being upfront and clear about financial expectations can not only begin to create a legacy, but can create a positive culture around money for future generations. Teaching them the basics, like what I teach in The Pressure-Free Money Course https://elleingalls.com/courses/pressure-free-money/ can help you and them all get on the same page: a balance sheet of all assets and liabilities that shows net worth, and a statement of all income and expenses with an easy budgeting process.

Your growing family. I was surveying women in their 40's-70's about stressors, and the third greatest stressor behind finances and the evening news, was their adult children. Marriages, divorces, financial problems, drug and alcohol problems, health issues, problems with grandchildren, or not having any grandchildren. The list went on and on. Life. There is always something! Many of these women said that parenting their adult children was far more difficult than when the children were small. I think it's because when grandchildren start coming, there is a deep-seated need to make sure the next generation flourishes.

There is so much you can't control. You can't control your adult child's sexuality, choice of mate, lifestyle, where they live, addiction. You can't control whether or not you will even have any grandchildren. When you feel yourself wanting to meddle, ask yourself, "How can I nurture and guide?" When you feel yourself acting in judgement, ask yourself, "How can I be helpful here?" When your children ask for help, ask yourself, "How can I best serve them in the long-term?" These empowering questions require peaceful thoughtfulness. Take your time answering them.

Nearly every extended family I know, including mine and my husband's, has members that don't exactly get along with each other, who don't understand each other, who don't talk to each other. It's ok to be at peace with that. And it is also ok to keep your heart soft for reconciliation at any time.

Documents. One of the biggest stressors for any family is when documents aren't in order. When I turned 18, my parents took me to the family lawyer's office and I wrote my first will. I left my bank accounts to my parents and my bicycle to one of my sisters. The bike got stolen when I went to college, and every scrap of money I had was spent on college, but I learned the importance of keeping your documents in order. Wills, trusts, power of attorney, bank accounts, retirement accounts, credit card accounts, just to name a few.

Create a contact list of all of the people in your life whom your family should know about like your attorney, your physicians, your dentists, your bankers, your brokers, and anyone who does business with you. A list of all your subscriptions for work and family and a safe place with all of your passwords is also helpful. CLEAR instructions for everything and everyone is important. And even with clear instructions, things can get muddy really fast. Make sure to update everything at least once a year.

Beyond your family. What causes and charities do each one of your family members care about? Do you tithe, and give? Do you volunteer and give your time? As you think about the potential impact your family can make on your extended family, your schools, your community, your state or province, your country, and the world, I encourage you to dream big. Someone has to! And you and your children have been given a unique set of talents and gifts to create something special on this planet. Whether that's a backyard garden and you share your tomatoes with the elderly couple who live next door, or an international organization where you go on a mission trip as a family.

The little things matter. "Will you put little presents under our kids' pillows someday?" One of my sons asked me this after my mother passed away. Little presents under their pillows was something she did when we visited or when she and Dad came to visit us. My sons wanted her legacy to live on through me with this simple act. What simple acts can you incorporate into your parenting and grandparenting that are legacy-worthy? How will you be remembered? Breaking the stress cycle is one of the greatest family legacies you can share with future generations.

Creating a family legacy
The future generations

- Developing financial success.
- Your growing family.
- Documents.
- Beyond your family.
- The little things matter.

Appendix i

YOUR PARENTING ACTION PLAN

Let's put an action plan together to help you take the steps you feel are important for the success of your family. Feel free to make copies of the worksheet on the next page.

Step 1. TARGETS Re-write your Target Chart specifically in terms of improving your family life.

Step 2. TRIGGERS Re-write your Trigger Chart. Think about all the ways you have overreacted in the past concerning the targets you've written down. For example if you get nervous for your child before events, a trigger could be *concerts, games, competitions,* or, *matches*. If you often yell for everyone to hurry up so that you aren't late to school, a trigger is *feeling we're going to be late*.

Step 3. TOOLS. What tools can you use in 10 seconds to prevent the release of stress hormones so that you can change your response from your old habit?

Step 4. IDENTIFY NEEDS What needs do you feel you could improve upon for your family?

Step 5. WRITING YOUR FUTURE. Clearly state your target on a goal sheet. (sample on next page) Use the *Write Your Future Everyday* tool from Chapter 3 to keep it fresh in your mind as you place actions on your to-do list, and qualify all the events of your day with inspiring words.

Step 5. CELEBRATE! How will you and your family celebrate your progress on your changes? Save money for a trip? Go for a hike? Get some jump ropes and sidewalk chalk? Make a special meal? Write down some ideas together.

MY #1 TARGET/GOAL/DREAM/VISION:

This is how achieving this goal will look, feel, smell, sound, taste to me:

I will accomplish my goal by this date:
The people and resources I need to make this happen include:

My strategies/tasks: **Date to be completed:**

The ways we will celebrate progress and completion of this goal are:

MY #2 TARGET/GOAL/DREAM/VISION:

This is how achieving this goal will look, feel, smell, sound, taste to me:

I will accomplish my goal by this date:
The people and resources I need to make this happen include:

My strategies/tasks: **Date to be completed:**

The ways we will celebrate progress and completion of this goal are:

MY #3 TARGET/GOAL/DREAM/VISION:

This is how achieving this goal will look, feel, smell, sound, taste to me:

I will accomplish my goal by this date:
The people and resources I need to make this happen include:

My strategies/tasks: **Date to be completed:**

The ways we will celebrate progress and completion of this goal are:

Notes:

APPENDIX ii

ACKNOWLEDGEMENTS

Many thanks to my husband Peter, my sons Hugh, Edmund "Ned", and William for allowing me to share stories about us. Check out their work at IngallsPictures.com.

Many thanks to Laurel Gaumer; Sandi Shine Ball; Debbie Vance; and Pam McConnell, UKCP, CTA for helping me edit and proof this book. If you find a typo or grammar error, that's my fault since I added more material after these dear friends read through my draft.

Thank you to Lisa Feinberg for sharing the "F" *Fib*, and Kathy Szenda Wilson for sharing the "F" *Fawn* with me. I've added those to the stress response list ever since you both shared them with me and it has helped many of my clients.

Many thanks to Robert G. Allen, the New York Times bestselling author, for his support of my writing this book, and for his willingness to write the foreword for it. I first met Robert in 2012 when I applied and was accepted into a mentorship program of his. This book would not have been possible without the many years I have immersed myself in his teachings. Through him I met Laurel Gaumer, my writing accountability partner, whom I am so grateful to know; I appreciate all of her help.

Thanks to all of the mentors, teachers, coaches and professors I have been so lucky to have known in my lifetime. Private music lessons were by far the most important learning experiences of my life, developing the discipline that carried over into my athletics, my career, the raising of our children, and the creation of Pressure-Free Living.

To the authors, psychologists and scientists on the following pages. I am grateful for all I have learned from their expertise, their creative endeavors, and from their research. I have read hundreds of books and research papers, and these are the key ones that have informed my work. If there is anything in this book that you would like more insight on, please contact us at Elle@Pressure-Free.com.

To you, the reader of this book, I sincerely thank you for taking the time to read this book. If even just one of the suggestions here makes a difference in your family's life, my heart is full. You are the reason why I wrote this book.

Appendix iii

Sources and Resources

The following are a compilation of sources and resources for this book:

- R. Bowen: Physiological Effects of Medullary Hormones, 1998.
- http://www.articlebase.com/health-articles/cortisol-is-a-corticosteroidhormone-1217552.html.
- Dr. Marianne Legato: video What is Cortisol and How Does it Affect Women After Arguing?, 2008.
- Robert Allen and Mark Victor Hansen: Cash in a Flash, Harmony Books, 2009.
- Lung health study: https://www.sciencedaily.com/releases/2018/02/180216084912.htm
- Hydration: https://www.medicaldaily.com/75-americans-may-suffer-chronic-dehydration-according-doctors-247393
- Will Bowen: A Complaint Free World: How to Stop Complaining and Start Enjoying the Life You've Always Wanted, Doubleday, 2007.
- Gregg Braden: The Divine Matrix: Bridging Time, Space, Miracles, and Belief, Hay House, 2007.
- Dawson Church, PhD: The Genie in Your Genes: Epigenetic Medicine and the New of Intention, Elite Books, 2007.
- Timothy Ferriss: The 4-Hour Work Week, Crown, 2007.

- Jim Collins: Good to Great: Why Some Companies Make the Leap... and Others Don't, HarperBusiness, 2001.
- Richard Gerber, MD: Vibrational Medicine: The #1 Handbook of Subtle-Energy Therapies, Bear and Company, 2001.
- Julia Hanna: Power Posing: Fake It Until You Make It, Harvard Business School Working Knowledge, September 20, 2010.
- Gay Hendricks: The Big Leap: Conquer Your Hidden Fear and Take Life to the Next Level, HarperOne, 2009.
- Napoleon Hill: Law of Success, Jeremy Tarcher/Penguin. 1928, 2008.
- Dr. Ben Lerner: Body By God, Thomas Nelson Publishers, 2003.
- Carrie McCarthy and Danielle LaPorte: Style Statement: Live by Your Own Design, Little, Brown and Company, 2008.
- Mark McCormack: What They Don't Teach You At Harvard Business School: Notes From A Street-Smart Executive, Bantam Books, 1984.
- Jason Selk: Ten Minute Toughness: The Mental Training Program for Winning Before the Game Begins, McGraw-Hill, 2008.
- Steven K. Scott: Simple Steps to Impossible Dreams: The 15 Power Secrets of the World's Most Successful People, Fireside, 1998.

- Brian Tracy: Goals! How to Get Everything You Want - Faster Than You Ever Thought Possible, Berrett-Koehler Publishers, 2003.
- Wallace Wattles: The Science of Being Rich, originally published in 1910, Barnes & Noble, 2007.
- Stuart Wilde: Life Was Never Meant to Be a Struggle, Hay House, 1987.
- Gary Keller with Jay Papasan: The One Thing, Bard Press, 2012.
- The Wisdom of Florence Scovel Shin, SOHO Books, 2017
- Dr. Joe Dispenza: Becoming Supernatural, Hay House, 2017
- Victoria Moran: Living a Charmed Life, Harper One 2009
- https://www.simplypsychology.org/maslow.html article on Maslow's Hierarchy of Needs
- Lila Veronica: TheLilaVeronica.com

For the video version of this book, copy and paste this link:

https://Pressure-FreeParenting.com

LET'S STAY CONNECTED!

Do you have a group of people who could benefit from learning the Pressure-Free Method? Let's find a time to talk and make it happen: SpeakWithElle.com

Join me on:

FaceBook: https://www.facebook.com/ElleIngallswithPressureFreeLiving

Instagram: https://www.instagram.com/elleingalls/

Linkedin: https://www.linkedin.com/in/pressurefreeliving/

Take a Do-It-Yourself Pressure-Free Course at ElleIngalls.com/Courses

Make Pressure-Free a part of your daily life with the Pressure-Free Planner and weekly trainings from all of Elle's courses:

Pressure-FreeU.com

Explore private coaching for you or one of your family members. Schedule a strategy session at SpeakWithElle.com

Online Courses by Elle Ingalls

http://elleingalls.com/courses/

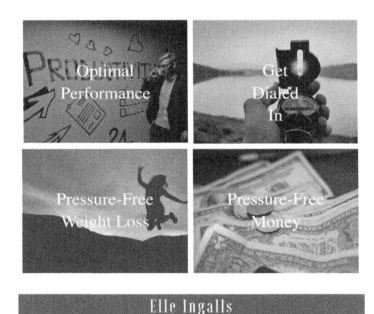

Made in the USA
Monee, IL
13 January 2021